NUNO FELT

Liz Clay

NUNO FELT

Techniques and inspiration for accessories and home interiors

A & C Black • London

First published in the UK by
A&C Black Publishers Ltd
36 Soho Square
London W1D 3QY

www.acblack.com

Reprinted 2008
Reprinted 2010

Text by **Liz Clay**
Photographs by **Shona Wood**
Design by **Lisa Tai**

Conceived and produced by Breslich & Foss Ltd.,
Unit 2A, Union Court, 20–22 Union Road, London SW4 6JP

A CIP catalogue record for this book is available from the British Library.

ISBN: 978-0-7136-8601-2

Printed in China

10 9 8 7 6 5 4 3

Contents

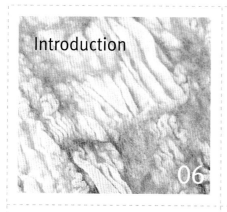

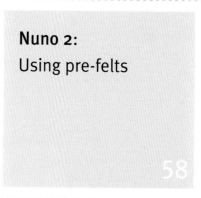
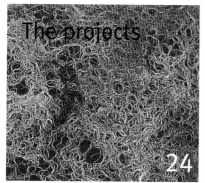
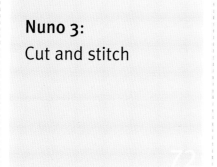
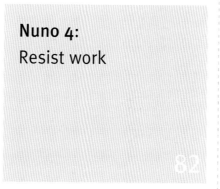

Introduction

My journey as a feltmaker began from a passion for applied arts in every conceivable form. Thanks to a formal textile background and a degree in Creative Arts (focused on weave and construction), it was no great surprise to find myself exploring felting techniques with woven materials. Nuno technique is a descriptive term that originates from the Japanese word *nuno*, meaning woven material. A thirst for discovery and innovation along with many happy accidents has resulted in thorough research in felted textures combining woven and non-woven materials. This book introduces a range of projects that explore established nuno techniques and methods closely related to them to show the versatility of textural effects possible in felt.

My personal response in using this technique reflects my love of nature. Much of my inspiration is gained from plant fibres and papermaking techniques. Organic forms such as leaves, rocks and bark, and the patterns and rhythms found in natural and manmade landscapes are also important sources of reference for my work. I am excited by the surface texture of felt and the 'edges' created by the juxtaposition of different materials. By mixing fabrics and fibres, the possibilities for textural landscapes are endless. I am particularly fascinated with the idea of felt

being light, transparent and gossamer both in touch and appearance. Much of my work involves many fine layers creating delicate lace like edges. Sensitive use of materials is an essential part of my creative process in making exclusive handmade products. Beyond the solitary confines of my studio, research and travel are essential to my practice. Cultural exchange and awareness of techniques are vital elements from which I make informed decisions.

I live and work on the edge of the Mendip Hills near Wells in Somerset, in the South West of England. My studio is in the garden next to open fields that look out across the Somerset Levels. The wool fibres I use are often sourced from local farms and then washed and processed by me. It's a time consuming and dirty process, but one that provides

Tulle Fantasy (page 53) combines the richly embroidered surface of a shop-bought scarf with fine merino wool.

In the Floral Silk Wrap (page 65), merino wool flowers are trapped between layers of silk chiffon.

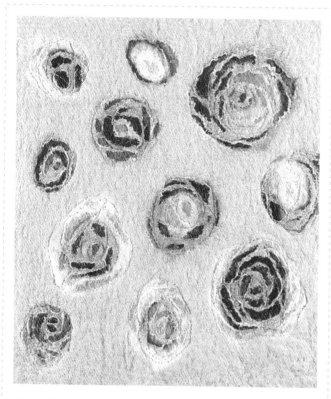

This pattern is just one of many variations of the cut and stitch technique explored on page 72.

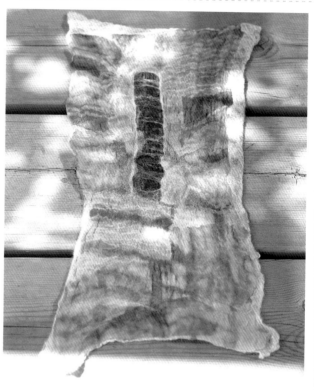

This delicate sample demonstrates the effect of layering silk chiffon with inserts of ribbon. (See page 117.)

a contextual link to the origins and history of this ancient craft. It is also a good starting point from which to explore the great versatility of felt.

Felting as a technique offers the textile designer a broad canvas of expression and endless creative opportunities. More explicitly the nuno technique offers rich rewards in design when combined with other textile applications and processes. Cross-fertilisation of methods can produce innovative and highly distinctive results for both the amateur and the more experienced felt maker alike.

Most of the techniques used in this book involve simple processes using basic household equipment. The skills required are not demanding and, with practice and creative planning, the student's only restriction is his or her own imagination.

Liz Clay

Getting started

The technique of nuno felt involves the entangling or binding of wool fibres with a woven structure. This process involves heat and friction. The result is a fabric that has undergone a structural change by manipulating the surface using the felt process. The basic technique requires only water, soap and a pair of hands. Beyond that, additional processes may be applied to the surface structure at considered times during the design process.

The book is clearly divided into sections that explain how to use these processes within individual projects. These include: pre-felts; cut and stitch; resist work; layering, and the use of additional materials and equipment including the embellishing machine. Throughout the text I've included helpful tips and suggestions to save you time. Additional ideas and inspiration is offered to encourage experimentation.

In this chapter you'll find a section on Finishing Processes. Step-by-step instructions are given for lining a scarf, making a cushion, using hanging supports and making buttons that can be used as fastenings for bags. General decorative finishes using 2-D and 3-D felt will be shown within individual projects.

Materials and equipment

Choosing woven fabrics

Natural fibres provide the most satisfactory partners with which to felt wool. The more open the weave construction the easier it is to make the wool fibres adhere during the felt process. Wool fibres need space to travel through the woven cloth. The combination of heat and friction creates the right environment for the felt process to work. As a guide, the closer and denser the weave structure of any fabric type, the more difficult successful felting will be. Having said that experimenting is always worthwhile!

NATURAL FIBRES

SILKS

There are many types of silk fabric available to buy cut from a roll or as ready-made hemmed items, such as scarfs. The appearance and drape will depend on the quality of the silk and the type of weave construction used in the manufacturing process. Silk has a wonderful luxurious look and feel, and a special translucent quality that is ideal for creating delicate, layered effects in nuno felt.

Chiffon This light, transparent fabric is very easy to felt onto, making it ideal to use in a first nuno project.

Silk georgette Similar to chiffon, georgette has a more textured surface but is slightly heavier.

Silk organza This is a denser weave of silk that has a slightly stiff quality to it.

Habotai or **pongee silk** A smooth textured silk that ranges from light to medium and heavyweight. It creates a light but very strong nuno felt that is suitable for clothing. Habotai silk dyes beautifully.

Shantung A fine to medium weight of silk, shantung has a delicate sheen. The weave is textured and has a slub effect that adds interest to the felted surface.

Silk tulle This net fabric is generally used for ballet wear and wedding veils.

COTTONS AND WOOL

Cottons are available in a wide range of fabric qualities. The soft, sheer, lightweight cottons are the most appropriate to use in nuno felt processes.

Muslin and **voile** Both are soft, smooth, semi-transparent, lightweight fabrics with an open weave.

Cotton lawn This has a slightly denser weave than muslin, but has a very soft drape.

Calico Calico is available in a range of weights and weave structures. Choose the lightest weight for a nuno project.

Scrim Usually dressed with size, scrim has a very open weave. It is available by the metre in various widths or as 6 cm (2½ in) width rolls from builders' merchants.

Hessian This is composed of jute fibres that are woven in various weights and qualities.

Wool muslin An open weave wool fabric, this material is light and soft to handle.

SYNTHETICS

Synthetic fabrics also make good bases for nuno work. Suitable materials include nylon, acrylic and polyester, and a range of mixed fibres: choose fabrics that don't have too dense a weave. It is also worth experimenting with nylon netting and lace fabrics.

···⫶ TIP FOR SUCCESSFUL FELTING

Use cold water first when felting wool fibres into fabric. Hot water will make the wool felt too quickly and before it has had a chance to entangle with the woven structure. My first encounter with nuno felt produced a beautiful lattice felt scarf completely separated from its silk chiffon base! However, this was a worthy result despite my intentions and the time spent laying out a carefully structured grid pattern. It's worth noting that fine layers of wool will felt into the woven fabric more easily than thicker layers, which can be another reason for the wool and fabric to part company.

← *Fabrics for nuno include: silks, cotton muslins, builders' scrim, open weave wool, nylons and lace.*

Materials for surface interest

The addition of other materials during the early stages of felting can add interesting visual and textural qualities to the finished felt surface. Natural fibres such as silk tops, flax, carded cotton, and other animal fibres (such as alpaca and mohair) work extremely well, integrating easily with the wool fibres during felting. Synthetic fibres and yarns may need trapping lightly with a fine layer of wool to encourage the bonding process. Hand carding and blending different fibres before laying onto the fabric base is another way to ensure successful adhesion during felting. Other materials may be trapped within or on the surface of the wool and fabric layers before felting begins. (Fabrics for use with an

↑ *A selection of fancy yarns in natural fibres and synthetic fibre blends, all of which are suitable for surface decoration. Tussah silk tops, flax fibre, ribbons, feathers, leaves, stones, sequins and lace.*

embellishing or needlepunch machine will be dealt with separately in Chapter 7.)

- Silk tops
- Yarns: all types
- Ribbons
- Fabric scraps
- Knitted fabrics
- Sequins and glitter
- Lace
- Feathers
- Leaves
- Found objects, including stones and shells

A word about wool

Most textile fibres possess the ability to matt to some extent, but animal fibres are the only fibres that can be felted satisfactorily. Wool is obtained almost exclusively from sheep, but other animals such as Kashmir goats are reared for their wool, known as cashmere. As with all animal fibres, wool fibres are made of proteins. Each protein is the product of a gene, which determines the structure and mechanical properties of wool fibre and is responsible for the variation in wool characteristics between sheep breeds. These protein fibres are covered with overlapping scales and when moisture, heat and friction are introduced the barbed fibres straighten. When cool, they spring back and lock together. This process is unique to protein fibres and is not reversible!

Sheep's wool is one of the easiest animal fibres to use in hand felting because of its unique ability to entangle and produce a matted or felted fabric. Wool is very resilient and elastic and the amount of crimp or curl in the fibre will determine the ease of felting. The 'crimp effect' is the main reason why a fine Merino fleece will felt more quickly and easily than a coarse and more hairy Herdwick fleece, for example. Wool can be stretched by up to one third of its length and it will spring back into shape. It can absorb moisture but repel water. There is no man-made material that can do all of this.

For projects that involve traditional wet feltmaking techniques wool is the essential ingredient. Other animal fibres, such as alpaca, mohair, angora, yak and camel, can be used successfully in feltmaking and create interesting results when blended with different wools. There are many different wool types worldwide and most will felt with some

← *Wool fibres: tops in various hand-dyed shades, natural shades of fleece wool and carded wool batts.*

degree of success depending on the wool type, the skill and experience of the feltmaker and the intended result required. There is not the space in this book to go into great depth regarding the pros and cons of using various wools. Here are some examples of wools in three basic fibre categories:

Coarse and straight: Herdwick, Swaledale, Icelandic
Medium and wavy: Cotswold, Masham, Jacob
Fine and crimped: Merino, Shetland, Blue Face Leicester

Wool that has coarse fibres has large flat scales while finer wool fibres contain a smaller scale structure. The latter is responsible for the crimp characteristic or wavy, springy performance of the fibre and adds to the 'crimp effect' in hand-felted processes. These wools are a good starting point, but I am always in favour of experimentation.

A vast choice of commercially produced natural or dyed wools is available to buy in various preparations. Washed fleece, combed tops, and carded batts in a myriad of colours and textures, including different blends containing other natural and synthetic fibres, are all easily sourced. As mentioned earlier, the finer wools are easier to handle and make a good starting point for the beginner feltmaker. They produce good results and a sense of achievement, which is especially important for children. However, there are many other qualities of wool that offer distinctive features, such as character and structure unique to the particular breed and it would be a great loss to the feltmaker to overlook the potential these wools can give in texture, colour and appearance in design applications. My advice is to be adventurous, give some unusual wools a try and increase your knowledge as your skills develop.

STORING YOUR FIBRES

Wool is best kept cool and dry in sealed cardboard boxes or paper sacks. These materials allow the wool to breathe. Never use polythene bags, as the wool will sweat. Wet or damp wool will deteriorate quickly. Watch out for moths and other insects that can damage and spoil the fibres.

A processed merino wool top is the favoured wool type of many feltmakers because it is fine quality wool that felts easily. Its fine quality makes merino fibre especially suitable for nuno felt work because the individual fibres require minimal persuasion to move easily through the weave of the fabric. The projects shown in this book use this wool. However, wherever possible I have suggested alternative types of wool fibre that will give rewarding and often surprising results. Experiment and have fun!

Everything from the kitchen cupboard!

Feltmakers are very resourceful creatures, possessing all manner of extraordinary objects both found and homemade in their feltmaking repertoire. It is essential to work at a good firm table at the right height. Working with water will create a damp atmosphere, so make sure your choice of room is suitable, especially the floor! Here are the essentials that I would recommend to get you started:

- Bubble wrap/sheeting/calico
- Net curtain fabric
- Sponge
- Olive oil soap
- Rubber mat
- Towels
- Reed blind or mat
- Plastic piping, 2–5 cm (¾–2 in) in diameter
- Plastic bowl
- Rubber gloves (if sensitive to wool and soap)

↑ *Basic feltmaking equipment includes: reed mat, length of plastic piping, net curtain, plastic bowl, rubber gloves, towel, hand carders, bubble wrap, sponge, olive oil soap and water spray container.*

Using dyes

Chapter 4 contains examples of nuno scarfs that employ the shibori dyeing method. To dye a fabric successfully it is important to identify its fibre content. In simple terms, fabric may be classified as having natural fibres – cellulose (from plants), protein (from animals) – or synthetic fibres (man made). However, hundreds of variations and combinations of these main fibre types are used in the manufacture of cloth worldwide so it is easy to understand how the use of dye might affect the final colour. This is particularly true when considering the differing fabric structure, weights of materials, and the undyed fibre states that are possible.

There is a wide range of fabric dyes and dye applications available from craft shops, and advice and information is easily found via websites and from books on the subject. As with fabrics, dyes vary enormously between the different brands. In addition, some dyes are more vivid on cellulose than protein fibres and vice versa so it is best to experiment on test pieces before beginning a project.

The dye resist projects in this book use fabrics made from natural fibres: silk and cotton. These two fabrics have a different fibre content and so require different methods of dyeing. For individual hand-dyed projects that involve using a dye bath or applying the dye with a brush or sponge, I recommend using both cold water dyes and cold water fibre-reactive dyes, which are available under a number of brand names. The dyes can be used safely within a domestic environment in small quantities. For good results and safety, it is essential to follow the manufacturer's instructions and always wear a face mask, gloves and protective clothing when using any synthetic dye powders. Remember to wash your fabrics before dyeing them to remove any size or dressing, grease and dirt which may not only affect the ability of the dye to fix but the final colour result, too. Dyes will react differently according to the base colours of your fabric, so test the dyes on a sample first.

···⟶ **TIP FOR NATURAL DYES**
Instant colour without the worry of toxic fumes can be achieved with food colourings, onion skins and tea bags! These are ideal for projects involving children, but with adult supervision because heat is required.

FOOD COLOURINGS
These work well with protein fibres such as silk and wool but will NOT colour cotton fibres. Soak the fabric, wool yarn or fibre in a solution of water and vinegar until the liquid is fully absorbed. Add food colouring to the shade required and heat then simmer for 10 to 15 minutes. Allow to cool then rinse the yarn or fibres with cold water.

TEA BAGS
Here's a good way to use up a pot of stewed tea! Black tea bags give a beautiful antique gold colour to silk fabrics, or try using herbal teas for an additional colour range. Place about 8 to 10 tea bags or 200 g (7 oz) of tea leaves in a pan with 500 ml (1 pint) of water, bring to the boil then simmer for 10

→ *Useful resist materials include: small stones, strong thread or string, elastic bands, marbles, buttons, dried pulses and clothes pegs.*

to 15 minutes. Allow to cool. Strain the liquid and put it in a clean pan with enough cold water to cover the fabric or fibres to be dyed. Bring slowly to the boil then simmer for approximately 45 to 60 minutes. Stir regularly to distribute the dye evenly over the fabric. Add more water if necessary to keep the fabric covered. Allow the fabric to cool in the dye bath, then remove and rinse well with cold water.

ONION SKINS
For richer shades of browns and yellows, boil approximately 200 g (7 oz) of onion skins using the same method as for tea bags. This works well on all fabric types and will result in a wide palette range depending on the amount of onion skins used and the fibre content of the fabric. But, be warned: red onion skins do not give a red dye!

These natural dye methods create a beautiful base colour to fabrics containing cellulose or protein fibres that may then be resist dyed using the various techniques shown in the projects.

···⟶ **TIP FOR DYEING WOOL**
Wool fibres are sensitive to high temperatures, but will not be harmed when simmering in a dye bath provided that the fibres are not agitated or stirred too vigorously. Always rinse and wash carefully when processing and avoid shocking the fibres with extremes of temperature.

Finishing methods

Many of the techniques used within the book may be applied to different end uses. After the step-by-step instructions, additional samples are illustrated that show the same methods, but use different materials. Basic finishing methods are shown below with further suggestions on adapting these. For example, the Cut and Stitch project on page 72 shows how to make a scarf, but the technique can also be used for a triptych wall hanging.

Lining a scarf

There are occasions when lining a felt scarf can enhance the appearance or add weight and drape to the decorated fabric. Nuno felt has qualities that exploit both sides of the manipulated surface and it would be a shame to lose one or the other by hiding a surface beneath a lining cloth. However, a beautiful hand-dyed silk or cotton fabric can complement and often improve the performance of a fabric for wearing or for use in interior design.

TOOLS AND MATERIALS
- **nuno scarf length**
- **hand-dyed habotai silk the same length as the scarf**
- **pins**
- **scissors**
- **needle and thread**

···⟩ **TIP FOR WASHING SCARFS**
Scarfs may be hand washed in a mild soap solution with luke warm water. Soak the scarf and gently squeeze the soapy water into the fabric. Rinse with clean water and dry flat on a towel. Never rub the surface or rinse fabrics vigorously by wringing. While still damp, press with an iron set on the silk setting. The silk gossamer scarfs (pages 27–45) can be left to dry naturally and should not require pressing. Scarfs with deep colours or strong dyes should be washed separately in case some colour bleeds.

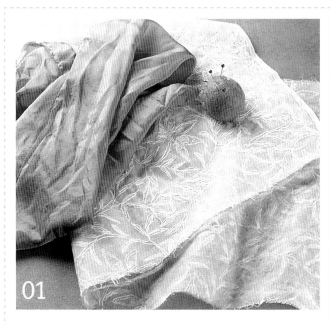

Choose a suitable weight of hand-dyed habotai silk fabric for the lining, cut to the same size as the scarf piece.

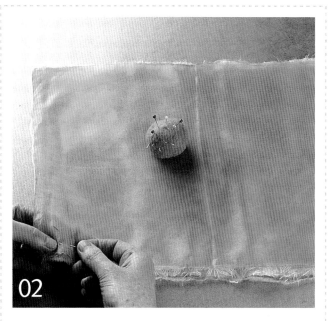

Press the fabrics using an iron on a gentle heat. Place the lining and felt pieces right sides together along all four sides, but leaving a 10 cm (4 in) opening in the middle of one of the short sides for turning in Step 4.

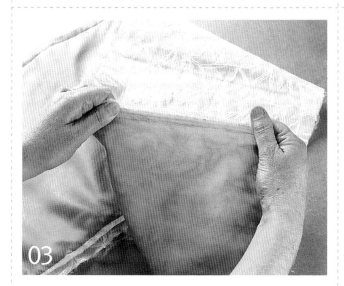

Machine sew around all four edges using straight stitch and remember to leave the opening open. Trim the seams to 5 mm (¼ in) and cut across each corner to reduce the bulk of the fabric. This will help to create a sharp edge to the corners of the finished scarf.

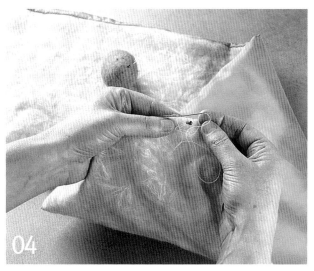

Turn the scarf inside out and slip stitch the opening closed with a needle and matching thread. Press with a warm iron.

Making a cushion

This is the simplest method to make a cushion, but it does not allow you to remove the pad without undoing the sewing. Choose more elaborate or decorative methods to close the cushion cover if removing the filling or pad is an important consideration. Zips, buttons, tapes, ribbons, hooks and press-studs may all be used as alternatives to the simple stitched fastening shown here.

TOOLS AND MATERIALS
- **nuno cushion panel**
- **cotton muslin the same size as the panel**
- **pins**
- **scissors**
- **cushion pad**
- **needle and thread**

Cut a piece of cotton muslin to the same size as the felt fabric. Pin the felt and lining fabrics with right sides together.

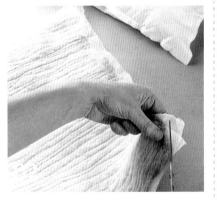

Machine sew using a straight stitch along three sides leaving a 15 cm (6 in) opening in the fourth side. Trim the seams to 5 mm (¼ in) and cut across each corner to reduce the fabric bulk. This will help to create a sharp edge to the corners of the finished cushion.

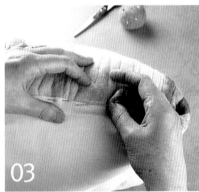

Turn the cushion cover inside out and press the seams with a cool iron. Place the cushion pad inside the cover and close the opening by pinning and then slip stitching by hand.

Preparing a wall hanging

Unframed felt work that is light and non-transparent may be fixed to the wall using batons or dowels made from wood or plastic that is pushed through a series of looped tapes sewn to the reverse side of the felt fabric. This method is simple and easy to do and will not damage the felt as the weight is evenly distributed across the width of the hanging. A baton may also be attached in this way to the bottom edge of a piece of felt to give weight and stability to the overall dimension.

Larger or heavier felt cloths may be fixed to walls using Velcro tape: hand stitch one side of the tape to the felt and glue the other to a baton that is screwed into the wall.

TOOLS AND MATERIALS
- **wall hanging**
- **strong cotton tape**
- **scissors**
- **pins**
- **needle and thread**
- **length of dowel or baton slightly wider than the wall hanging**

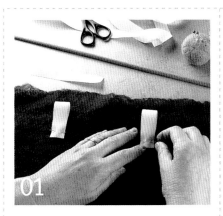

01

02

03

Cut enough pieces of tape for the length of the hanging. A piece every 10 cm (4 in) along the top is usually adequate. Cut each piece of tape to 10 cm (4 in) in length and fold into a loop. Pin each loop to the top edge of the felt work, leaving a 2 cm (1¾ in) gap above each loop.

Hand stitch each tape to the felt using running stitches across the width of each loop at 1 cm (½ in) and 3 cm (1¼ in) from the lower unfolded edge. Take care that the stitches do not show on the right side of the felt.

Push the dowel or baton through the loops. The wall hanging is now ready to be hung.

Buttons and trimmings

There are many complementary materials that work well with felt and have a decorative or functional purpose. For example, leather and wood can offer both strength and a sympathetic surface quality when combined with felted wool. Contemporary feltmakers are continually pushing the boundaries and experimenting by combining felt with glass, plastics, metals and other new materials to create innovative and exciting products. However, I often find the best and simplest solution to creating fastenings or trimmings is found using felt itself.

Felt trimmings are often more appropriate and successful in partnering a hand-felted item. Not only is it easy to match colour or blend suitable fibres, but you can make the exact size or shape of fastening required. A very attractive and functional trimming can easily be made using a felted sausage shape that is sliced into buttons. I have used foil in this design to add a touch of glamour and a jewel-like quality to the buttons. However, as foil cannot be felted, I added a backing to the button slices to secure the foil layers within and retain the button shape.

TOOLS AND MATERIALS
- assorted materials such as merino wool tops, fabric scraps, yarns, aluminium foil
- bubble wrap
- olive oil soap
- scissors
- knife
- heavy-duty cotton fabric or leather
- fabric glue

Choose your materials and colours. These can include merino wool tops in various shades, scraps of silk fabrics and yarns, and recycled wrappers from confectionery and chocolate bars.

Pull two pieces of different coloured wool fibres from the length of the tops. Slightly wet the bubble wrap surface and rub with the bar of soap.

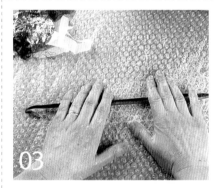

Lay the strips of wool together lengthways and roll on the bubble wrap until they form a narrow sausage shape. Wrap fabric scraps around the wool sausage; roll firmly and add another layer of wool and then more fabric if required. Yarn may also be added at this stage.

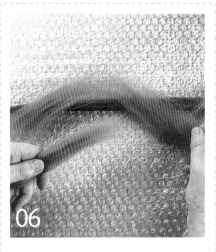

Lay the felt sausage into a length of another colour of wool top and roll up, adding soap and water as necessary. The silk fabric adds colour and texture, but also helps bind the sausage tightly and firmly.

Add sections of aluminium foil and squeeze gently around the wool sausage shape.

Add further contrasting layers of wool. To create irregular colour marks in the final button design, place the wool in curves along the sausage length.

Continue to build up the layers of wool, aluminium foil, and silk scraps until the roll is 1.5 cm (¾ in) in diameter. The final layer of wool should be thick enough to completely cover all the inside layers. Roll the sausage firmly, using hot water to encourage the felt process, until it feels firm and hard. Leave to dry over night in a warm place.

With a sharp knife, slice the felt sausage into buttons 5 mm (¼ in) thick.

To add strength and durability, cut button size circles in heavy-duty cotton fabric or leather and attach these to the flat surface of one side of each button using fabric glue.

The projects

Nuno 1: Exploring texture
Step-by-step project: Gossamer scarf

Nuno 2: Using pre-felts
Step-by-step project: Edge-to-edge book cover

Nuno 3: Cut and stitch
Step-by-step project: Cut flowers scarf

Nuno 4: Resist work
Step-by-step project: Bubble scarf

Nuno 5: Layering
Step-by-step project: Pebble bag

Nuno 6: Haberdashery
Step-by-step project: Silk yarn wrap

Nuno 7: Embellishing
Step-by-step projects: Cushion cover and Gaudi brooches

Nuno 1: Exploring texture

There are many fabulous ways to decorate a length of fabric using the nuno felt technique and create a very special scarf. Depending on the amount of fibres added to the base fabric and the amount of felting used, the appearance and feel of the scarf may range from light and gossamer to a more structured and weighty drape. The possibilities are endless and once the basic skills are understood an exciting journey of fun and creativity can begin.

Silk fabrics possibly offer the most satisfaction in creating a luxurious quality both in look and feel. However, there is great potential in using fine cotton muslins and synthetic fabrics, too. In choosing the suitability of a fabric for the nuno technique, look carefully at its weave structure. It should not be dense or closely woven. That said I am always in favour of experimenting with a fabric to see what might happen!

Arranging the wool fibres randomly over the surface before felting begins will result in an abstract design. More structured and considered designs are possible using pre-felted wool cut into shapes and then felted into the fabric. The final result will depend on the amount of fabric surface area covered with the additional fibres and the degree to which these have been felted. A fine, even covering of wool will give a softer more rippled effect. Spacing between the added wool fibres will create wonderful surface patterns, as the fabric is pulled and ruched as the wool felts. A puckered and seersucker effect can be achieved in this way.

tools and materials

- 10 g (½ oz) merino wool tops
- silk chiffon scarf with rolled edges, 30 x 145 cm (1 x 5 ft)
- bubble wrap, the same size as the scarf
- 5 g (¼ oz) tussah silk tops
- net, the same size as the scarf
- sponge
- bowl for water
- olive oil soap

making a sample

As with any new technique, taking the time to make a sample will save valuable time and expense in the long run. This is particularly true when using costly fabrics and fibres. Scale is an important factor when making samples. It is fairly difficult to understand what results can be achieved using very small sample pieces of fabric. I recommend that you experiment on pieces at least 40 x 40 cm (15½ x 15½ in) in order to ascertain how the fibres and fabric will work together. This will also give you a sense of the visual impact of the nuno effect and the potential it offers for design.

→ *The Gossamer Scarf is – as its description suggests – a light, transparent and featherweight accessory.*

>> **EXPLORING TEXTURE**/ GOSSAMER SCARF

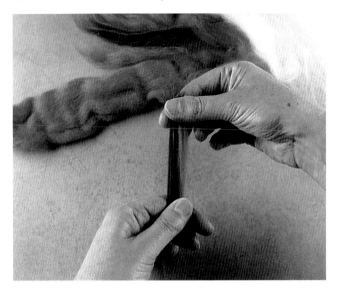

1 Mix the merino wool tops to create your own range of colours. To do this, take small lengths of wool approximately 5–6 cm (2–2½ in) and mix them between thumbs and index fingers using a pulling action.

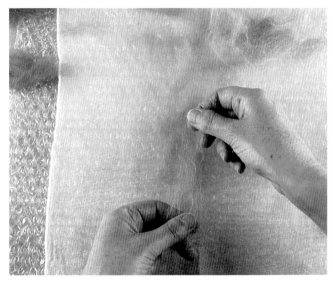

2 Place the scarf, right side up, onto the length of bubble wrap, bubble side up. Lay two or three fine layers of merino wool and tussah silk fibres over the scarf surface in a random pattern.

3 Cover the entire scarf and bubble wrap with the net, then gently wet the surface with warm water using the sponge. Push the sponge firmly into the net, working from one end to the other.

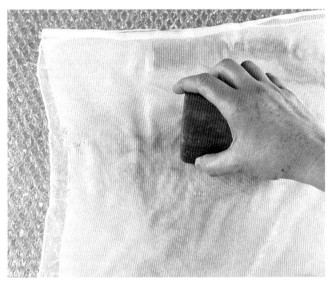

4 Rub the soap smoothly across the entire surface of the net, making sure no dry areas remain. Using your hands, work the soap and water into the wool and fabric through the net for a couple of minutes.

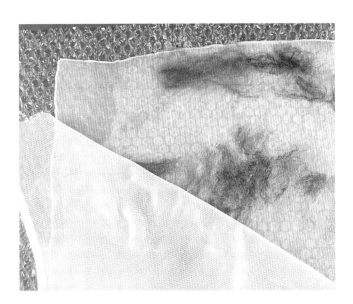

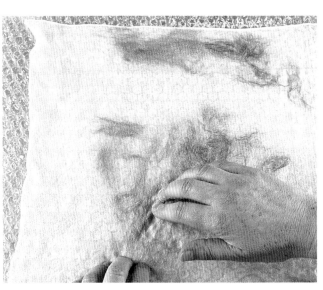

5 Gently peel back the net starting at one corner. The added wool and silk fibres should remain on the silk scarf, but gently reposition any that lift away.

6 Rub the wool into the scarf with your fingers, increasing the pressure as the wool begins to adhere to the silk chiffon. Carefully turn over the scarf and continue rubbing from the other side.

7 After three or four minutes rinse the scarf in clean water and gently squeeze out any excess. Check the surface by gently pulling the felted areas between thumb and forefinger to see how well the wool has attached. The surface will be quite fluffy at this stage. Carry on rubbing with added soap and water until the wool becomes matted and is completely fixed to the scarf.

8 During the final stages of the felting process, you will notice the silk chiffon become ruched and puckered in the areas where the wool has not penetrated. The more friction that is applied to the fibres, the tighter and more textured the surface will become.

Silk chiffon scarfs collection

The gossamer appearance and feel of these scarfs is created using transparent silk chiffon fabric that is felted with merino wool and silk tops. There are various ways to apply the merino and silk tops to the fabric, each of which will create very different effects.

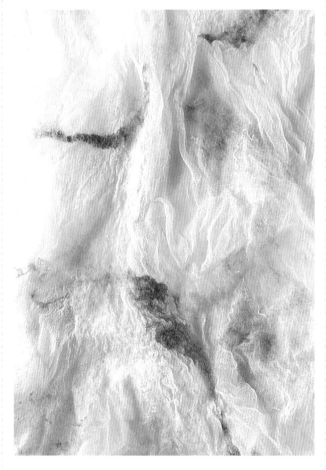

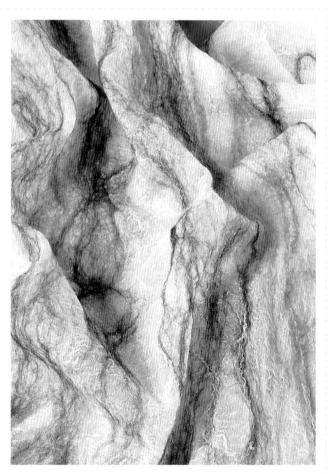

White and grey gossamer scarf
Above *This gossamer scarf uses georgette fabric, a sheer crepe silk that is heavier than chiffon and has a crinkled, textured surface.*

Red gossamer scarf
Above and right *A cut length of silk chiffon was covered in a fine web of dyed merino and silk tops to create this scarf. Take a length of merino and silk top that is 20 cm (8 in) longer than the scarf length. Gently open out the fibres widthways into a fine web without breaking the fibre length. The fibre web should cover the entire surface of the scarf. After felting, the result will be the lovely marble effect shown here.*

SILK SAMPLES / CHIFFON

Midnight scarf

Left *A cut length of silk chiffon is completely covered with a layer of finger-carded merino wool. Once felting begins, the wool separates into a cracked effect. Further felting will result in a denser effect and a thicker fabric. If the eventual length and width of the scarf is important to you, cut a larger piece of fabric to allow for extra shrinkage. Experiment on a sample of chiffon first.*

❖··· TIP FOR SUCCESSFUL FELTING

The amount of felting – that is, how hard you work the fibres and for how long – will determine the final appearance of a nuno scarf. The more friction applied to the wool fibres the greater reduction there will be in the surface area of the fabric as it is taken up in the felt process. This will happen with any fabric type. Different end results can be achieved using the same materials simply by varying these conditions.

Marbled scarf

Above *This length of silk chiffon is covered with finely spaced wisps of wool pulled from the merino tops. This technique results in a very subtle marble effect.*

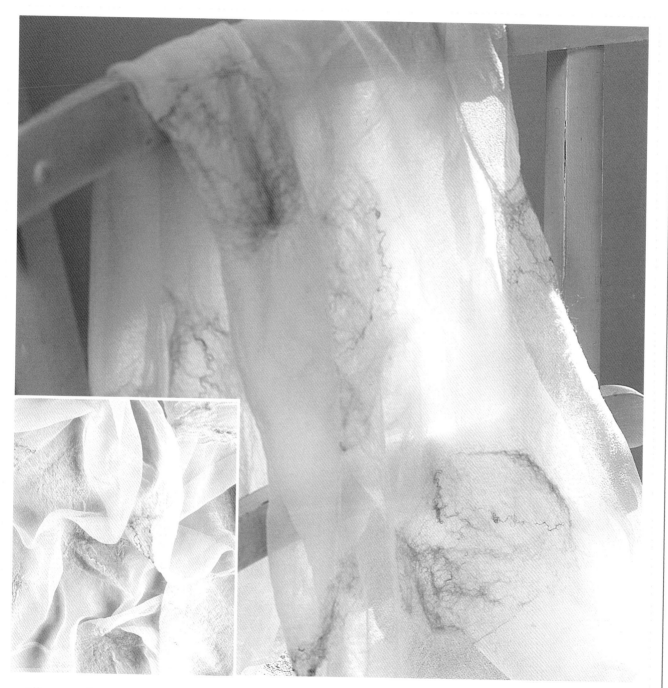

Lilac sample

Above *In this pretty sample, short lengths of dyed silk and merino tops were gently pulled open into a fine web and arranged on the silk base fabric, leaving empty spaces between each web.*

⚬⋯ TIP FOR NEATENING EDGES

When using cut fabric pieces, felting the wool fibres into the cut edge seals the raw edges of the fabric.

>> **SILK SAMPLES** / CHIFFON

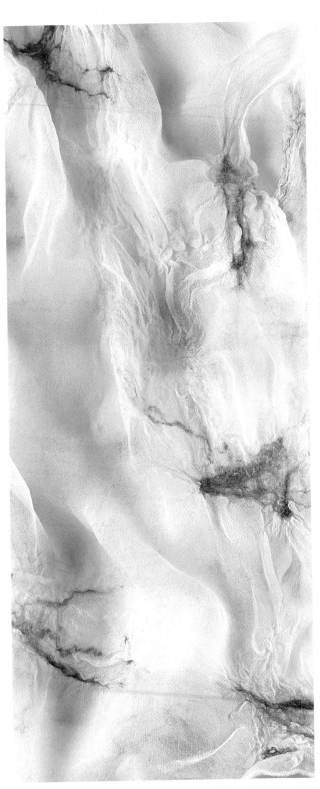

Blue gossamer scarf
Above *A more considered design element was used on this cut length of silk chiffon. Thicker strips of merino and silk tops were laid at random angles to cover one side of the chiffon fabric.*

Mint green gossamer scarf
Left *Painting onto the silk fabric before felting can create striking and subtle effects. Here, a bought silk scarf with ready rolled edges was first painted with pale green stripes, applied with a paintbrush. Once dry, merino wool and silk fibres were felted into the fabric.*

Pink cushion
Right *This pretty cushion is made up from a richly textured felt cloth. I used silk and flax fibres hand carded and felted into a dyed merino pre-felt with a silk chiffon base.*

SILK SAMPLES / CHIFFON

Lined scarf collection
Above and right *A sumptuous collection of textured silk scarfs with hand-dyed silk linings. Cotton, linen and silk fibres were hand carded with dyed merino tops and felted into a silk chiffon base. Each is lined separately.*

Habotai or silk pongee scarfs collection

Habotai or pongee is a plain woven, thin, smooth-textured silk fabric that is available in different weights. When used for nuno felt, this silk fabric makes a very strong but lightweight fabric that gives a slight bubble effect to the surface. Habotai is slightly more difficult to felt into than silk chiffon, but the results are very different and make wonderful scarfs and fabric for garments.

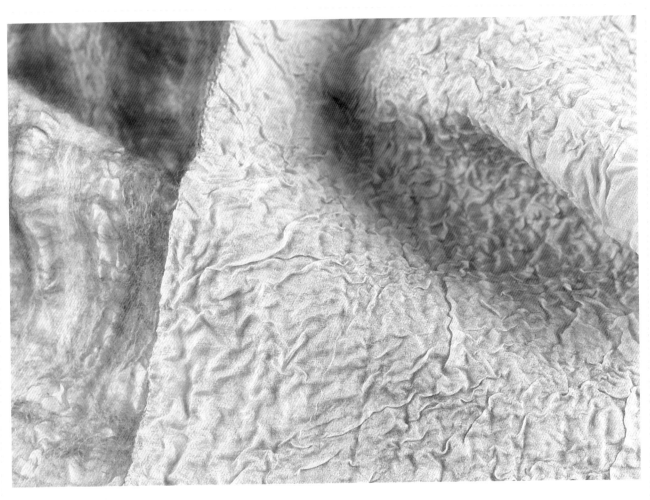

Highland heather scarf
Above and right *Dyed merino and silk tops were laid out in a tartan effect on one side of the fabric to create a distinctive scarf design with contrasting surfaces. Use a cut length of habotai silk or buy a ready rolled edge scarf. The lightest weight of fabric is easiest to use.*

SILK SAMPLES / HABOTAI OR SILK PONGEE

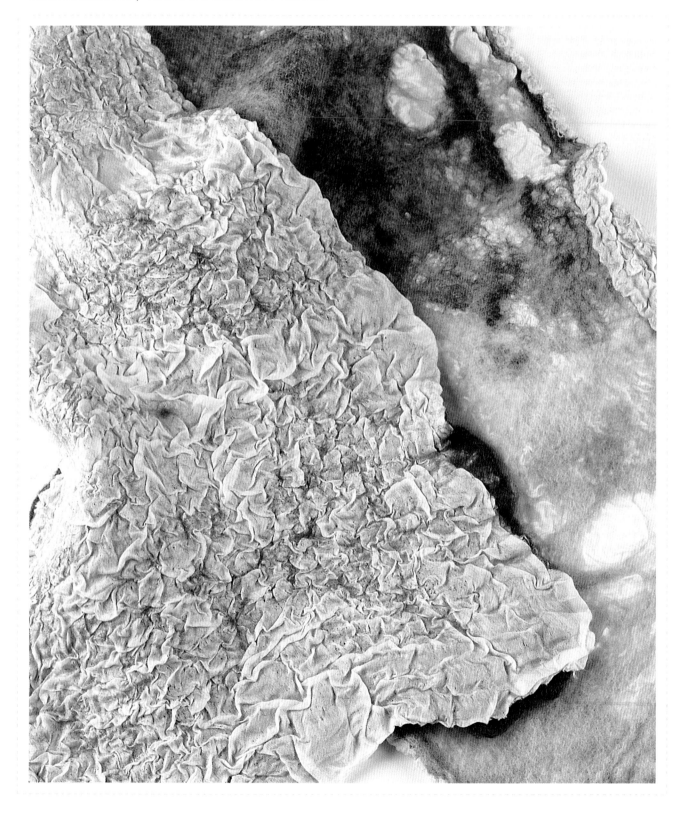

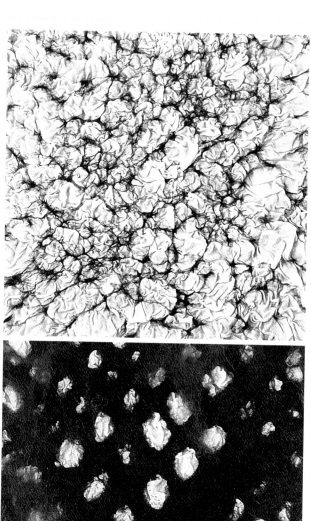

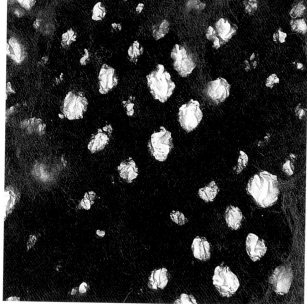

Sample fabric mix

Left and above *This selection of nuno felt using habotai silk fabrics demonstrates the different effects that can be created using coloured wools and different spacing of fibres.*

Criss-cross samples

Above and top *Laying tufts of merino wool in a criss-cross pattern with even spaces throughout creates a deliberate lattice effect. These samples were heavily felted to make a highly textured nuno felt on one side and a smooth wool surface on the other side. The finished cloth can be cut without the worry of frayed edges.*

Shantung silk scarfs collection

Shantung is a fine to medium-weight silk fabric also known as raw or tussah silk. (Tussah means wild.) It is a beautifully textured silk that is irregular in appearance and has a slightly crisp feel that will soften with washing. Shantung is not as lustrous as the cultivated silks and has a delicate sheen. The slub effect adds interest to its surface. These qualities make it more of a challenge to use in nuno felt but the result is certainly worth the effort.

Shantung silk scarfs are available to buy in a myriad of colours, including graded tonal effects. Use these as a base fabric to create beautiful textured scarfs that have a luxurious quality.

Lavender scarf
Above *Merino wool tops were laid in a very fine layer to cover one side of the shantung fabric completely. The fibres were then felted into the fabric until the surface began to crinkle and it became more textured.*

Rich walnut wrap
Above and right *To recreate this luxurious wrap, use a complementary colour of merino and silk tops and pull short tufts from the top length. Open up these tufts by gently pulling the fibres out in a web and lay them randomly in very thin wisps across the entire fabric surface. Felt lightly until the wool fibres have attached in a web-like structure across the fabric surface.*

>> **SILK SAMPLES** / SHANTUNG SILK

Red circles scarf

Above *Form circles of merino wool fibres and felt these into the silk fabric. Use both sides of the scarf for your design if you wish. For a more subtle all-over effect, felt the circles on one side only then fold the scarf lengthways, keeping the wool surface inside. Slip stitch the edges, leaving the fringed ends open so that you have a tube scarf. This is a good way to use vibrant wool colours to make a subtle nuno effect on the reverse side of a cloth as the design will appear more faint and shadow like.*

Gossamer chiffon and shantung scarfs

Right *These gossamer silk scarfs demonstrate some of the different effects and textures possible using merino and silk fibres. The central scarf is made from shantung silk, while the two outer scarfs use silk chiffon.*

Cotton muslin collection

Muslin is a sheer to coarse woven cotton fabric that is available in natural or dyed colours. It is an ideal fabric to use for nuno felt processes and satisfying results can be easily achieved.

Raspberry ripple scarf
Above *To create this 'raspberry ripple' effect, lay narrow strips of merino fibres in one direction randomly across the muslin surface. Vary the strips in length and thickness, giving some a tapered look. Felting along the length of the fabric following the linear design will create a ruched effect.*

Blue and red abstract scarf
Right *In this example, tufts of coloured merino tops in various shapes were used to create an abstract design. Strips, swirls, dots and circles were spaced out or overlapped to cover the muslin. The random layout of the wool fibres pulls the fabric in all directions during felting to create a textured and highly decorative surface.*

COTTON SAMPLES / MUSLIN

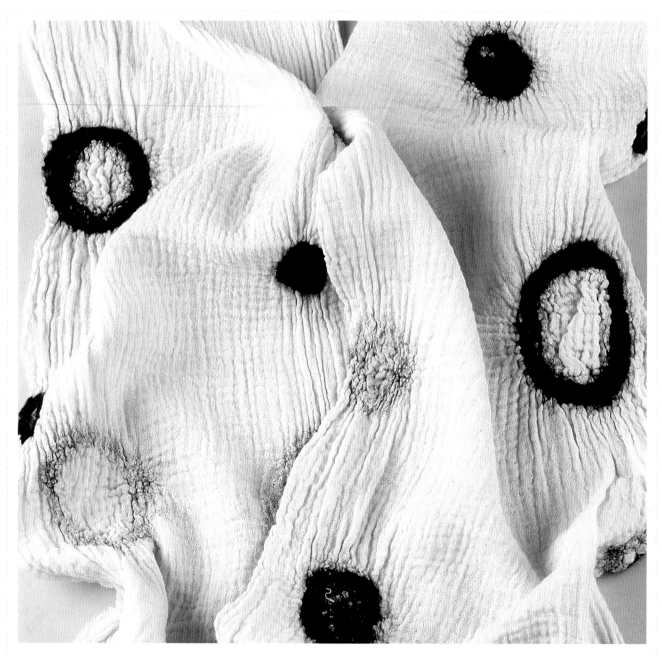

Circles scarfs

Above and right *This is a very effective use of the nuno technique that exploits the tonal qualities of felted surfaces by making a sandwich of muslin and felted shapes. Prepare the merino fibres in circles or dots and place these along half the length of the muslin. Fold over the muslin lengthways and put more wool shapes into any empty spaces. Felt these layers together. Muslin cloth is a very light fabric and can be layered without causing too much bulk. This method of folding and trapping felted shapes within and outside the cloth gives the muslin a satisfying weight and feel, which is especially good for scarfs. There is lots of potential for easily achievable texture and lively tonal effects in this technique.*

COTTON SAMPLES / MUSLIN

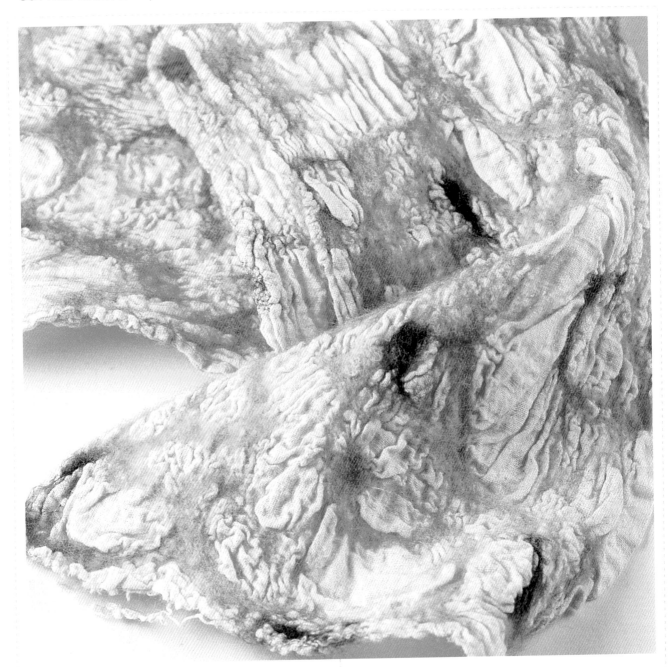

Apricot swirl scarf
Above *This scarf is similar to the Blue and Red Abstract Scarf on page 47, but more space was left between the wool shapes in this design.*

Greetings card collection
Right *Making simple cards is a wonderful way to use up small scraps of treasured nuno or your samples and experiments with fabrics and fibres. The cards can also be framed to make very special gifts or to become display features in your home.*

Synthetic fabrics collection

These fabric types are slightly more challenging to felt with and results are often less rewarding than natural materials, mostly from an aesthetic point of view in look and feel. However, they do offer a new and varied palette to work with that can provide great design potential.

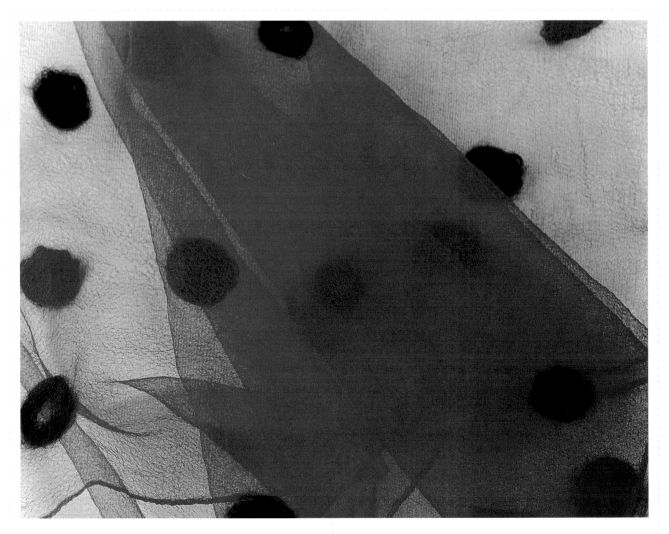

Polka dot scarf
Above *This nylon chiffon scarf has finger-carded merino spots applied to both sides. Putting the wool fibres on both sides of synthetic fabrics helps encourage the felting process: as the wool penetrates through the weave it felts to itself and traps the synthetic fabric in between.*

Tulle fantasy scarf
Right *This frothy delicate scarf has been given the nuno treatment with white merino tops. The richly embroidered surface of the original scarf undergoes further transformation and embellishment with the felt process.*

SYNTHETIC SAMPLES

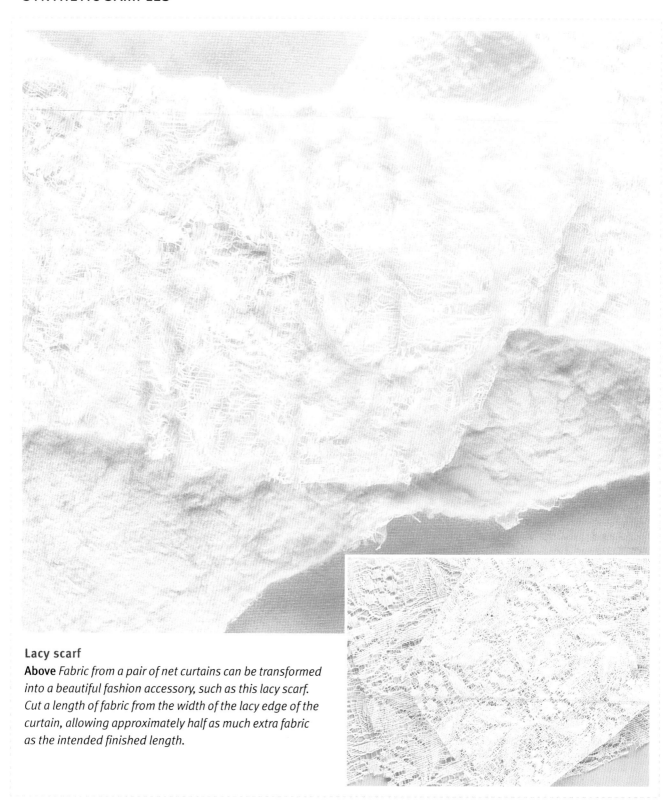

Lacy scarf

Above *Fabric from a pair of net curtains can be transformed into a beautiful fashion accessory, such as this lacy scarf. Cut a length of fabric from the width of the lacy edge of the curtain, allowing approximately half as much extra fabric as the intended finished length.*

Above *This photograph shows the felted surface of the wool side of the Lacy scarf.*

Left and inset *The picture (left) shows the felted surface of the scarf on the wool side, while the inset picture shows what the base fabric looked like.*

❖··· TIP FOR SYNTHETIC LACE

Felting merino wool into synthetic lace fabric creates a wonderfully textured surface that is strong and durable. Very pretty wedding accessories, such as bags, cummerbunds and hats, can be made with this inexpensive fabric.

SYNTHETIC SAMPLES

Hat trim

Above and right *Black silk chiffon was felted with dyed merino wool spaced unevenly along the length. The finished piece was gathered along the centre length to make a frill to go around a hat. Vary the width of the silk chiffon to make wider frills or stitch and gather two or three strips together to make gloriously frilly statements. Attach these strips to the neckline of dresses, blouses or cuffs.*

Nuno 2: Using pre-felts

Wool fibres undergo a series of transformations during the felting process. After the first wetting out and rubbing with soap, the fibres begin to entangle and form a sheet that is soft and unstable. This is known as the pre-felt stage. It is possible to carefully rinse the excess soap from the pre-felt and dry the cloth to be used later. Shapes and patterns may be cut from pre-felted cloth and be incorporated into project designs by adding them to the surface of fabrics or onto wool fibres before felting continues. Striking design effects can be produced using contrasting colours and exploiting the cut edges of the pre-felted cloth with fabric. (See for example the Muslin Square Scarf on page 67.)

Silk is used to enhance the design elements of the Edge-to-Edge Book Cover by adding depth, shade and contour. The approach is more subtle and the fabric surface is less disturbed by the felt process than it would be without the silk.

In this section, you will find suggestions for combining cut pieces of pre-felted cloth with silk chiffon and muslin fabrics. However, any of the nuno techniques featured in this book may be applied to this simple book cover idea; it just depends on the amount of surface embellishment desired and the design features used.

tools and material

To cover two books approximately 15 x 20 cm (6 x 8 in)

- 15 g (¾ oz) each of four contrasting colours of merino wool tops
- 15 g (¾ oz) extra of one colour for backing
- 25 cm (10 in) square of silk chiffon
- bubble wrap, 75 x 75 cm (30 x 30 in)
- net, the same size as the bubble wrap
- sponge
- bowl for water
- olive oil soap
- scissors

measuring your book

The Edge-to-Edge Book Cover is made in one single piece of felt. Before you make a cover for your book, you will need to measure it. Begin by measuring the height of the book and adding 4 cm (1½ in) to allow for shrinkage; this measurement will be the finished width of the felt piece. Open up the book and measure it from edge-to-edge, including the spine and front and back covers. Add half as much again to allow for the overlap required and the shrinkage. This measurement will be the finished length of your felt piece.

→ *Making a felted cover is an attractive way to protect books, photograph albums and other special bound collections. Letters may also be applied to the cover using the pre-felt technique, so you could add the book title or personalise the cover with the recipient's name.*

USING PRE-FELTS / EDGE-TO-EDGE BOOK COVER

1 Lay the first layer of fibres pulled from the merino tops on the bubble wrap, bubble side up. Keep the fibres in one direction in overlapping rows to form a squarish shape, 25 x 20 cm (10 x 8 in). Lay a second layer of fibres at right angles to the first layer. Repeat the process four times until you have a wool sandwich of four alternating layers.

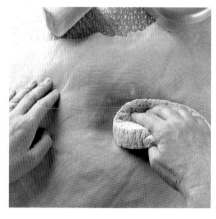

2 Cover the fibres with the net and carefully wet out using the sponge. Start at the centre of the square and work out towards the edges.

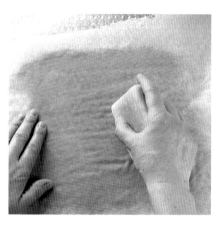

3 Rub soap across the entire surface through the net. Firmly and gently rub the soapy water into the fibres making sure that no area is missed. Remove the net by carefully lifting it away from one corner.

4 Continue to rub the wool surface with your fingertips for a further minute or two, gently increasing the pressure as the wool fibres become entangled.

5 Fold the pre-felt into a small parcel and rinse in clean, cold water. Keeping the parcel contained in your hand, carefully squeeze out the excess water.

6 Repeat this process with each colour of merino fibre. Dry and press the pre-felts ready to be used.

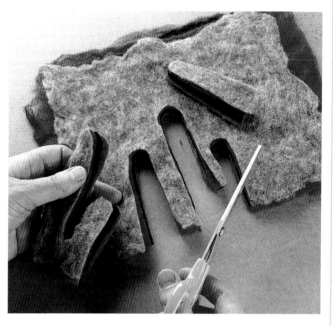

7 Stack the pre-felts into a sandwich of alternating colours and cut through the layers using scissors to create the required shapes.

8 It is important to keep the layers still when cutting and to make clean sharp cuts with the scissors, avoiding jagged edges or any movement.

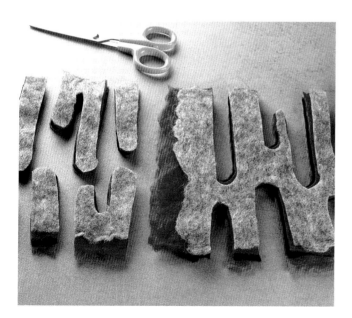

9 After cutting the design you will have a set of positive and negative shapes in each colour.

10 Next comes the creative part! Re-form the shapes into four complete sheets by choosing a two-tone design or a combination of all the colours.

>> **USING PRE-FELTS** / EDGE-TO-EDGE BOOK COVER

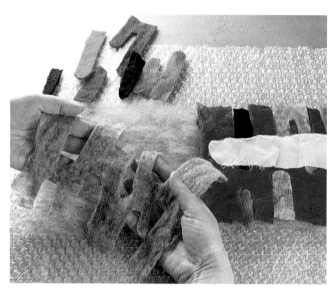

11 Place two pairs of pre-felt sheets next to each other along their short sides and slightly overlapping. Cut narrow shapes from the silk chiffon fabric and place these onto the cut pre-felt surface.

12 To add extra strength and support to the cut edges I recommend laying the sheets onto a bed of wool fibres. (This should be a single layer only.) Doing this will give a very different appearance to one side of the finished felt. (See Step 17.)

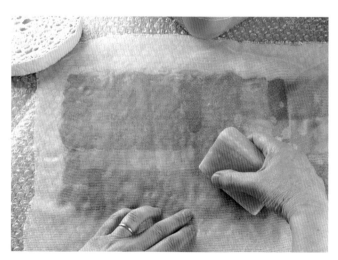

13 With either method you will have one side that features the silk design integrated with the cut pre-felts. Before the final felting process it is extremely important to ensure that the cut edges are pushed up close to each other with no gaps showing.

14 Cover the pre-felt design with the net and wet out the fibres very carefully with the sponge, making sure that you do not disturb the layout below. Rub soap over the surface of the net.

15 Rub very gently until the soapy water is completely absorbed and then carefully remove the net.

16 The felt will be very fragile and vulnerable at this stage. Working slowly and methodically, carefully massage the edges of the shapes together, encouraging them to bond. Patience is required! Do not be tempted to lift the felt too soon.

17 If you have added a single layer of wool beneath the pre-felts, bonding will take place more quickly. Gently lift the corner and fold back to see the progress made. If not fully felted, continue to rub the surface as you did in Step 16.

Here you can see the finished result using carded fibres in different colours on the reverse side. Without the carded fibres or a single layer of merino tops, the two sides would look the same and resemble the folded corner in the picture.

18 Make a felt strap that is long enough to be folded double, three times the length of the cover. (See Steps 2 and 3 of Buttons and Trimmings on pages 22–23, but use only one shade of wool.) Pin a loop in the centre approximately 10 cm (4 in) from the short edge of the cover. Stitch in place.

19 Wrap the book inside the felt cover and secure by tying the strap through the loop.

Using pre-felts

For defined edges and mark marking, cut shapes from pre-felts using sharp scissors. To create a more subtle effect with softer edges, use individually made pre-felted shapes that don't need to be cut out. The Floral Wrap (right) uses the first method and the Pink Mix Sample (below) uses the second.

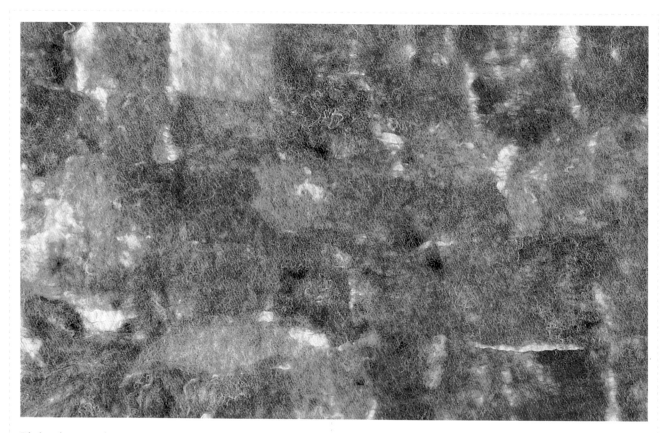

Pink mix sample
Above *Here hand-carded wool and silk fibres were pre-felted into individual square shapes and assembled in a chequered layer to cover a piece of habotai silk. Depending on the thickness of the wool, this design could make a light felted scarf or a more sturdy cloth to use as a book cover or to be turned into decorative cuffs, collars or pockets for garments.*

Silk floral wrap
Right *To make a floral wrap, lay out a single layer of merino and silk tops to make a very fine sheet of pre-felted wool. Cut flowers and petal shapes from this and assemble them on a length of silk chiffon or silk georgette. Cover with another length of silk fabric then felt the surfaces together. To add depth and a touch of reality to the flowers, layer fine webs of contrasting layers of coloured wool in a painterly fashion to each petal. You can also paint the silk beforehand with a flower design to echo the felt flowers.*

USING PRE-FELTS

Daisy bag
Left *This charming little shoulder bag is decorated with handmade linen and silk paper flowers and has a twisted cotton cord strap. Three layers of merino wool were felted into cotton muslin fabric to form the bag itself, which is lined with cotton muslin.*

Muslin square scarf
Above *Solid blocks of brightly coloured pre-felt squares create a striking fabric that can be used to make bags, cushions, table mats or table runners. The subtle reverse side of the fabric is equally attractive, as shown overleaf.*

>> **USING PRE-FELTS**

 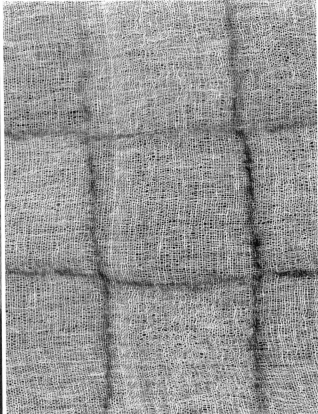

Pink and red scarf
Above left and right *A thicker pre-felt was used in bright colours on muslin cloth to create this scarf length. The strong vibrant colours become muted and appear pastel on the reverse side (above right). The cut edges of the pre-felted squares create wonderful blurred lines on the muslin surface, revealing just a hint of the true wool colours.*

Picnic blanket
Right *To create this cosy blanket, pre-felted squares were cut from large pieces of contrasting colours then reassembled into a chequered design on silk chiffon. The pre-felts should be made with no more than two layers of wool to keep a soft quality to the finished cloth.*

>> USING PRE-FELTS

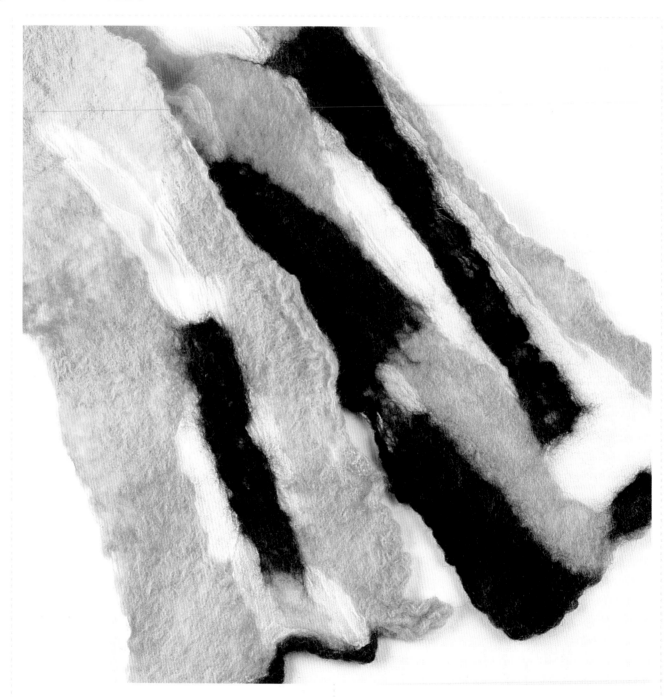

Yellow and black abstract scarf
Above *In this scarf, abstract shapes were cut from a sheet of pre-felted dyed wool in two colours. The cut out pre-felt was then felted into a matching length of silk chiffon fabric.*

Edge-to-edge wall hanging
Right *This wall hanging is a larger version of the pre-felt design used in the Edge-to-Edge Book Cover on page 58. A nylon chiffon scarf was used instead of silk, the rolled edge of which creates a subtle pencil line effect.*

Nuno 3: Cut and stitch

Felt is a wonderful fabric to cut and slice into, as there is no fraying of the edges. This unique quality makes possible quite precise patterns and considered design effects. Applied to nuno felt, the cut work technique creates choices ranging from subtle effects to dramatic and bold statements in design. To make the best use of this technique a painterly approach is needed when working with the wool fibres. By finger carding small amounts of dyed wool to 'paint' with, you can create your very own paintbox of colours. A muted palette will give a cohesive statement to the finished work. On the other hand, bold gestures using strong contrasts of colour will lend a very different feel to the end result. These decisions need to be made before felting begins so that maximum use can be made of the cutting process.

Alternatively, you can place pre-felt pieces onto the base layer of wool before the silk. This will lead to further exciting design effects once the silk is cut. Cutting away areas of the top fabric should enhance the shapes below, creating a shadow effect between the two layers.

tools and materials

- silk chiffon, 30 x 30 cm (1 ft x 1 ft)
- bubble wrap, 40 x 40 cm (15½ x 15½ in)
- merino wool tops, 30 g (1 oz) in green or your chosen base colour
- net, the same size as the silk chiffon
- sponge
- bowl for water
- olive oil soap
- 2 cm (¾ in) diameter plastic piping, 30 cm (1 ft) in length
- merino wool tops, 10 g (⅓ oz) in contrasting colours for the flowers
- sewing machine
- white sewing thread
- embroidery scissors

using embroidery

In the Cut Flowers series of scarfs, hidden layers of felted wool are revealed by carefully cutting away the top layer of silk fabric. Machine embroidery is used to enhance the design motif before the silk is cut. This combination of free machine embroidery with the cut work technique gives the finished piece a depth and beauty of tonal range with a subtle sculptural effect. The design shown in this sample may equally be applied to accessories, such as bags, or to home interior pieces, such as cushion covers and larger wall pieces.

← *Silk and merino nuno felt with stitched and cut embellishment. This example features subtle autumn shades.*

→ *The areas of cutwork contrast with the muted areas still covered with silk chiffon. A combination of cut and uncut flowers adds interest to the final scarf.*

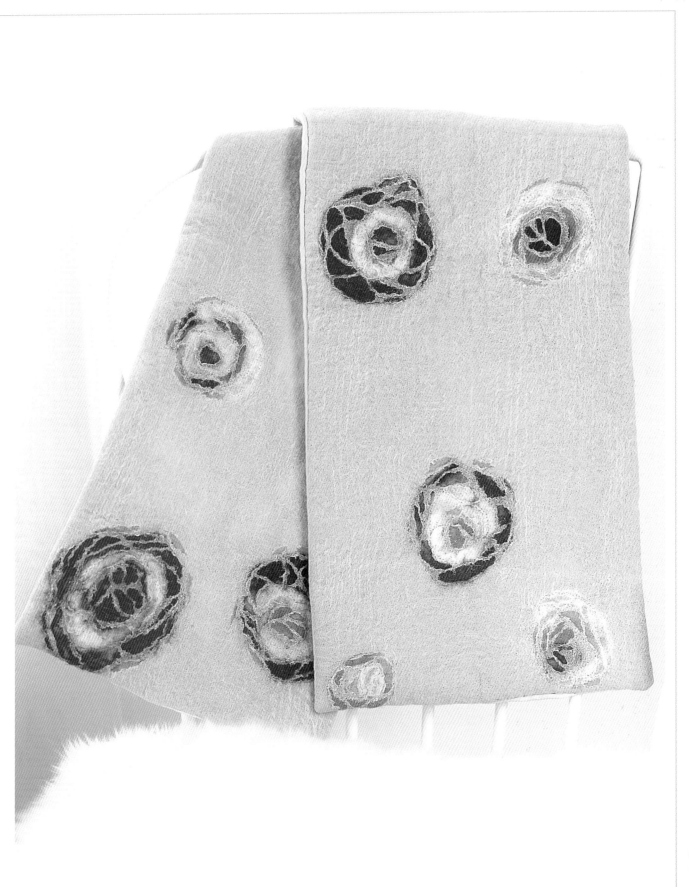

CUT AND STITCH / CUT FLOWERS SCARF

1 Place the silk chiffon on the work surface and cover it with the bubble wrap, bubble side up. (The piece of silk will act as a template for your sample.) Finger card the green merino wool tops and position them on the bubble wrap in two layers at an angle of 90 degrees to each other. Cover the area of silk chiffon visible beneath the bubble wrap, keeping carefully to the correct size.

2 Cover the layers of wool with net and wet the fibres with warm water using the sponge and working from the centre of the net outwards. Rub soap smoothly over the entire surface of the net.

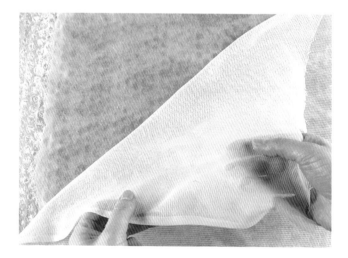

3 Gently rub the soap and water into the wool and silk with your finger tips for several minutes, then carefully peel back the net starting from one corner.

4 Roll the wool and bubble wrap around the plastic piping. (Set aside the silk chiffon for use in Step 7.) Roll firmly for about two minutes, checking occasionally to ensure that the surface of the wool has not become too wrinkled and the felt is stable and adhering to itself.

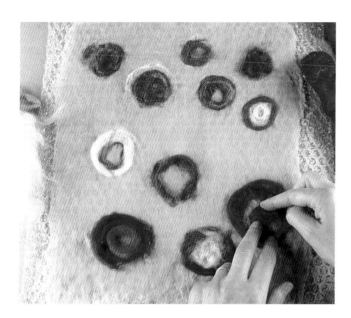

5 Unfold the felt and bubble wrap and remove the piping. Gently smooth the surface flat with your fingers. Using the wool tops in contrasting colours, lay circles of wool in different sizes over the base layer. Further mix colours by finger carding the yarns. Place the wool in lengths or carded tufts to create variety.

6 When you are happy with the design, cover the wool surface with the piece of silk chiffon discarded in Step 4. Wet the chiffon with soapy water using the sponge and working from the centre outwards.

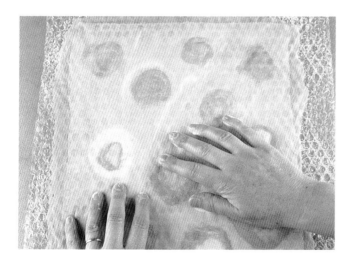

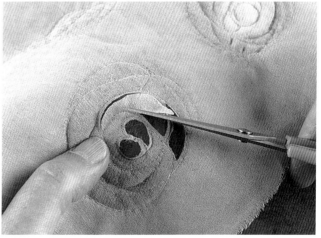

7 Rub the surface evenly with your fingers, taking care not to disturb the silk or the flower design beneath. Continue rubbing until the wool begins to adhere to the silk chiffon. When the wool has completely adhered to the silk, rinse the piece in clean, cold water and leave to dry overnight. Press with a warm iron.

8 Set the sewing machine to the free embroidery stitch and stitch petal shapes over each circle. Starting from the centre of each circle, increase the size of the petals as you move to the outside edge. Use the embroidery scissors to cut away the silk fabric from the felt following the inside edge of the stitching line. Take care not to cut too close to the stitches. The silk will lift away with a gentle pull. Continue to cut until the flower is complete.

Using the sewing machine

Simple running stitches can make very effective patterns that also strengthen the fabric. They can also be invisible when combined with cutting techniques. Machine stitches will stabilise a delicate frayed edge of silk chiffon and can also be disguised by it.

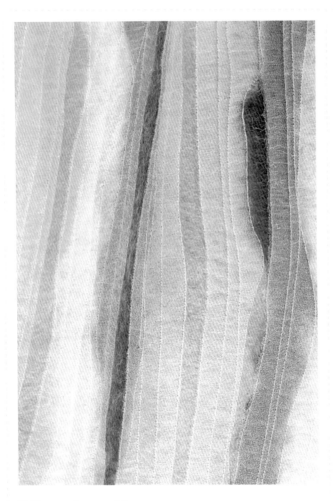

Yellow stripe cushion cover
Above *Various widths of different coloured strips of cut pre-felts were felted into a silk chiffon square to create this cushion cover. Rows were machine stitched through the felted fabric following the coloured stripe design, then selected strips of silk fabric were carefully cut away between the stitched rows.*

Frilly pink scarf
To create this fun scarf, cover a layer of pre-felted dyed wool in different colours with a layer of pink silk chiffon then lightly felt them together. Machine stitch across the width in even rows along the entire scarf length. Avoiding the felt surface, cut through the silk chiffon across the width between each row of stitching. Gather each row of stitches and secure them at each end to create a ruffled effect.

Zig-zag wall panels
Subtle earthy tones of felted wool with overlays of cut silk
chiffon create these evocative panels.

CUT AND STITCH SAMPLES

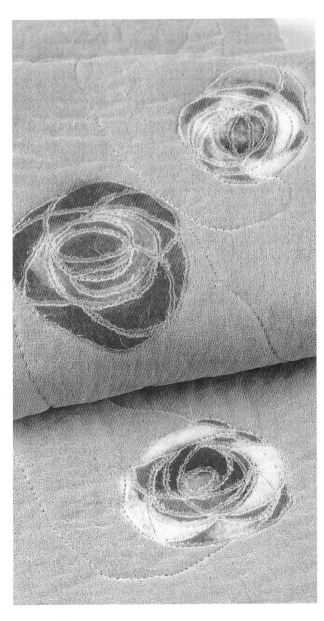

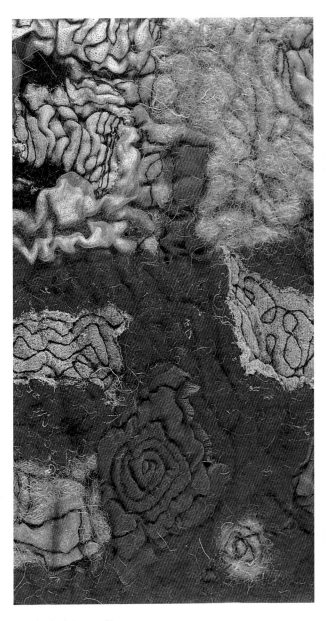

Orange flowers

Above *In this scarf from my Cut Flowers range, hints of citrus colours are embedded in layers of sumptuous silk fabric in matching tones.*

Pink flowers

Left *Hot pink, red and orange make a truly eye-catching combination.*

Study in blue collage

Above *This highly textured nuno sampler uses different fabric scraps of both natural and synthetic fibres that were machine stitched onto the pre-felted surface and then hand felted together.*

>> CUT AND STITCH SAMPLES

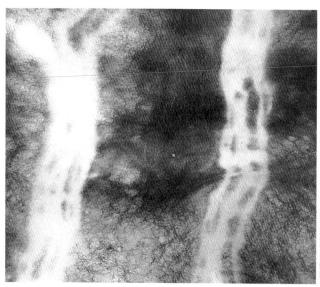

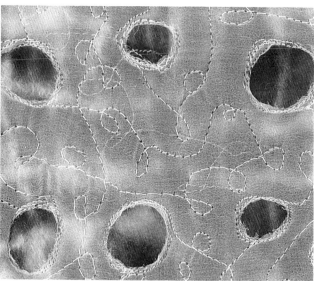

Shibori samples
Above left and right *This white wool pre-felt shows mark making that was created after being wrapped and dyed.*

Here silk chiffon was felted into the shibori sample (left). The machine-stitched design was then cut away to show circles of colour.

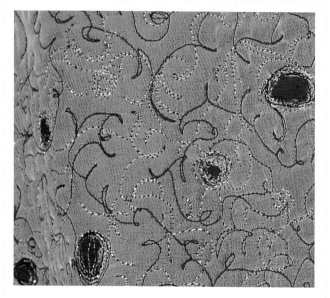

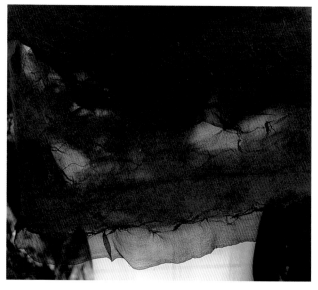

Red and gold embroidered sample
Above *In this example, a silk chiffon and pre-felt base was felted together then decorated with machine stitching in gold. Areas of fabric were then cut away and further stitching was added. A richly embellished cloth such as this can be used to add decorative features to garments.*

Black and maroon wrap
Above and right *This silk chiffon wrap was ruched with free machine embroidery stitching before being felted on one side with a single layer of merino tops.*

Nuno 4: Resist work

When a fabric surface is wrapped, folded, stitched or secured tightly, the covered areas are protected from dye penetration or other applications, such as felting. This is known as resist work and the degree of resist depends on the method, preparation and control of the resist material. For example, a thick strong cotton thread will resist dye far more efficiently than a soft wool yarn. Decisions must be made beforehand about the final effect required, although spontaneity will always be a key feature when working in this way.

Simple tie-dyeing or the more refined and precise techniques of Japanese shibori combined with the unique felting ability of wool fibres can produce stunning effects. The combination of dyes and resist methods to make marks on fabrics that will subsequently be used in nuno felt further increases the wonderful effects possible. An element of the unexpected is always present!

What is even more exciting is the manipulation of these embellished fabrics combined with the felt process. Shaping and securing the cloth with resists before dyeing creates the patterned surface of the fabric. These methods additionally create a unique three-dimensional structure to the surface when the resists are removed after drying. But, felting into the fabric before the resists are removed will fix the surface structure and enable further textural qualities of the surface to remain. This is particularly useful for wearable items that require washing, as the shape and textures would suffer and be easily destroyed when made wet.

tools and material

- resist shapes, such as buttons and marbles
- elastic bands or strong thread
- pre-dyed lightweight silk habotai scarf with rolled edges, 45 x 180 cm (18 in x 5 ft 8 in)
- 10 g (⅓ oz) merino wool tops and silk tops
- bubble wrap, the same size as the scarf
- net, the same size as the scarf
- sponge
- bowl for water
- olive oil soap
- strong thread, twine or elastic bands
- tea bag dye (see page 16 for the recipe)

dyeing with tea bags

The subtle dye effects of the Bubble Scarf were created using a dye bath of tea bags soaked in boiling water. The silk habotai fabric was dyed a soft pink before the resists were added, then finally soaked in the tea bag solution. For more on dyeing with both natural and commercial dyes, see page 16.

→ *The Bubble Scarf is an eye-catching and striking accessory that is both durable and easy to care for.*

>> RESIST WORK / BUBBLE SCARF

1 Choose from a selection of suitable resist materials, such as marbles, buttons, stones or dried pulses. You'll also need elastic bands or strong thread and a pre-dyed silk scarf length.

2 Wrap a section of the pre-dyed silk scarf around the chosen resist material and use an elastic band or thread to secure the material tightly and keep the resist enclosed. Repeat until the surface of the scarf is covered with a random pattern.

3 Wet the scarf with water, then immerse it in the tea bag dye bath for approximately 30 minutes. Remove the scarf and wring out excess liquid.

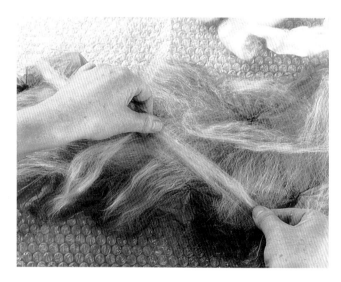

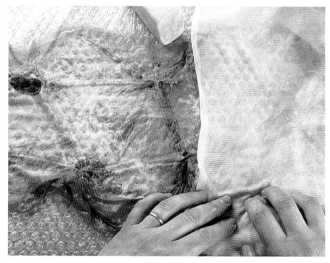

4 Lay the scarf open on the bubble wrap (bubble side up) with the covered part of the resist against the bubbles. Carefully lay short tufts of merino and silk tops across the scarf at angles in a criss-cross pattern. Completely cover the folds and flat areas of the scarf, but allow the tied openings of the resist areas to remain uncovered.

5 Cover with the net and add water and soap. Remove the net carefully once the fibres have fully absorbed the water and are stable.

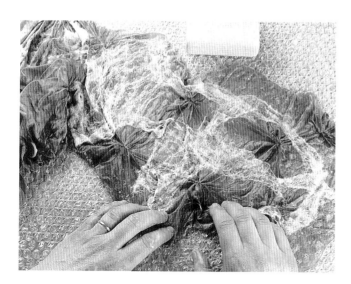

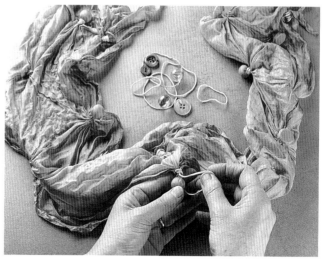

6 Gently rub the surface and gradually increase the pressure as the fibres begin to work through the fabric. As the wool becomes entangled and shrinks, the fabric will become more puckered and reduced in overall dimension. When felting is complete rinse the fabric to remove the soap and dye the scarf in a contrasting or complementary colour.

7 When the fabric is completely dry (usually after about 24 hours) untie the elastic bands or thread and remove the resist materials.

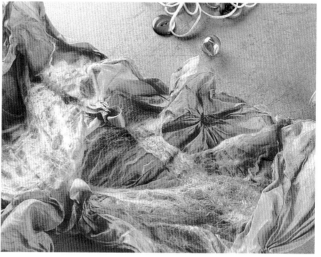

8 Depending on the dyes chosen the resisted areas will reveal subtle or strong contrasts of colour. If you have followed the tea bag method, the contrast will be a subtle one, as shown here.

9 The felted areas will trap the 'bubble' effect caused by the resists arranged across the scarf length.

Pre-dyed fabrics

A simple way to apply resist patterns to a cloth before felting is to use the tie and dye method. In this technique, sections of cloth are folded or scrunched into points and then tightly secured with string or elastic bands. The bundle is then immersed in a dye vat and the resists removed once the fabric has dried.

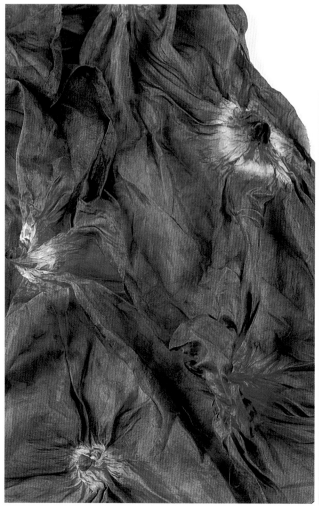 

Dyed scarf lengths
Above left and right *These fabulous designs were created using simple tie-dye techniques. Build up the intensity of colour by overdyeing and retying the resists to create slightly shifting patterns.*

Resist samples

Above *These pre-dyed samples demonstrate the effects of the many resist methods that can be used. These include folding and clamping with wooden blocks; wrapping with different thicknesses of string and thread or with widths of elastic bands; tying around materials such as stones, marbles and buttons; and securing folded cloth with pegs and paperclips.*

Shibori collection

On the following pages is a range of shibori dyed scarfs that demonstrate the effect of different resist methods on habotai silk. These include wrapping techniques that offer free expression of mark-making as well as the more precise method of folding cloth and clamping with shaped blocks of wood before dyeing.

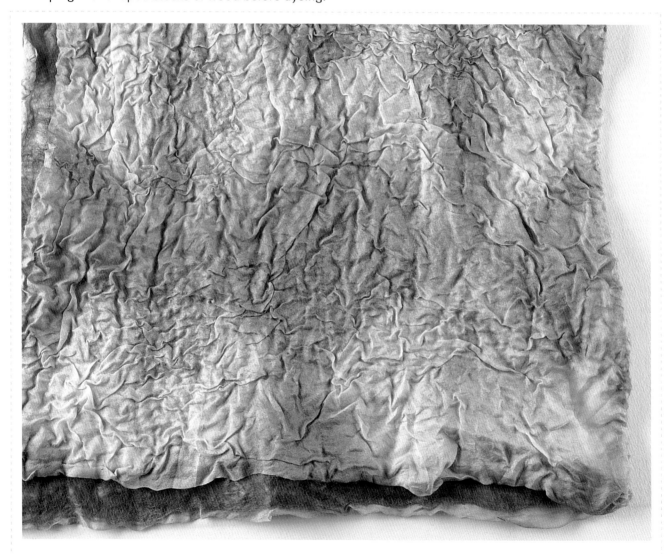

Above and right *Before felting, this scarf length was folded lengthways in four folds then clamped between triangular blocks of wood and dyed. The result is a bold geometric pattern on one side and a softer pattern on the other.*

SHIBORI SAMPLES

Left *In these designs, considered mark-making was applied to the habotai silk fabric before the felting process began.*

···⫶ **TIP FOR WASHING SHIBORI SCARFS**
Silk shibori designs require care during washing. To avoid the 'bubbles' and other raised surfaces collapsing during washing, it is advisable to replace the resists and tie them as securely as they were when dyed. After washing, leave the scarf to dry completely then remove the resists. If you don't have the original resists, similar shaped objects often work well enough. Alternatively, soak the scarf in a mild soap solution and carefully rinse, leaving to dry naturally. Never iron a scarf with a raised surface, or you will lose the effect! Scarfs with deep colours or strong dyes should be washed separately in case some colour bleeds.

Above *This silk habotai scarf was block resist dyed first then felted with merino wool to create finely textured folds and ripples of fabric in the surface.*

Above *In this example, the scarf was felted with merino wool before the resists were added. After tying and dyeing, areas of the felted wool were 'resisted' to produce subtle shading within the folds of the cloth.*

Above *Using a fine thread to wrap fingers of silk cloth produced cobweb patterns in this ruched, deep blue scarf.*

⟫ SHIBORI SAMPLES

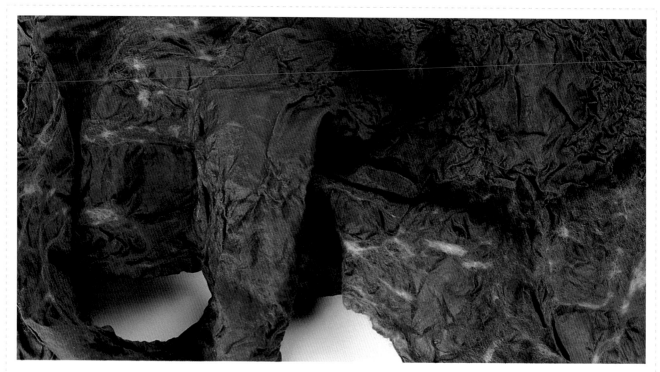

Above *Subtle hints of undyed felt and silk fabric emerge throughout this intensely dyed indigo scarf, producing a hint of China blue hues.*

Left and right *This gossamer scarf has subtle resist marks beneath its orange and red surfaces. Clever use of over-dyeing can result in the most unlikely colour combinations blending harmoniously.*

⋯⟡ TIP FOR USING PRINTS

Use commercially printed silks and cotton fabrics for additional impact combined with your own mark-making techniques. For example, add circular patterns to printed stripes. If using several colours, begin with the palest shade and graduate to darker shades to ensure the best results.

Nuno 5: Layering

The illusion of depth and a sense of landscape can be achieved very successfully by layering fine fabrics with wool fibres. An advantage of this method is that it allows objects that would otherwise not be easily felted to be featured in the design. I often collect beautiful stones and pebbles on my walks, and the seashore is always a good source of material. An exhibition brief once inspired me to use such finds. The challenge for me was how to incorporate a collection of pebbles within the felted surface without using glue or stitch. The simple answer was fabric. A degree of planning and carefully chosen fabrics can give very satisfactory results. Fine silk chiffons work very well indeed, as they become almost invisible when felted. The level of visibility will of course depend on the fabric colour and the tonal qualities of the pebbles or stones used. Silk chiffon adheres quickly when felted with wool fibres and provides an excellent bond for the trapped materials used. Care should be taken when selecting objects: sharp or jagged edges may tear the silk fabric during felting or indeed damage your fingers.

The shape used for the Pebble Bag can easily be used for a number of projects. For example, it makes a good tea cosy! Once you have mastered the technique, you can experiment with your own template shapes for bags and other useful vessels.

tools and material

To make a bag approximately 19 cm (7 ½ in) wide and 17 cm (6½ in) deep

- a selection of small pebbles
- 30 g (1 oz) each of two natural shades of Shetland wool tops
- 10 x 10 cm (4 x 4 in) black silk chiffon
- bubble wrap or plastic sheet 20 x 20 cm (8 x 8 in) for the template
- reed mat approx. 45 x 35 cm (18 x 14 in)
- net, large enough to cover the reed mat
- olive oil soap
- bowl for water
- scissors

choosing wool

It is often a good idea to experiment with different wool types when making bags or containers. There are some excellent qualities that will offer a greater strength and resilience than merino and definitely have more character. In addition you can create interesting colour effects and exploit surface textures by combining contrasting shades of the same or different wools. For example, using alpaca on the inside of a bag and merino wool on the outside creates a soft hairy surface where the long smooth alpaca fibres travel through the denser merino felt and emerge to create a hazy effect. This is especially attractive when the fibres are in different colours.

→ *The Pebble Bag is a worthy result of your labours: a robust little bag with a wholly original decorative surface.*

▶▶ LAYERING/ PEBBLE BAG

Cut a template from bubble wrap or a sheet of plastic. As the wool fibres used to make the bag will shrink during the felting process, make the template slightly bigger than you would like your finished bag to be. An extra 2 cm (¾ in) should be adequate for a Pebble Bag.

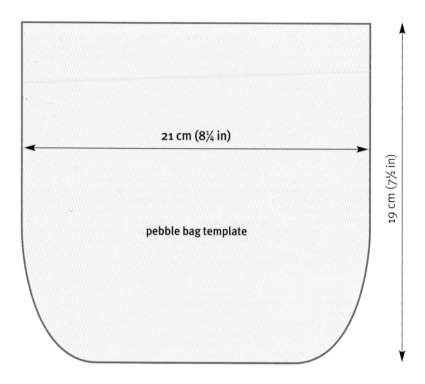

21 cm (8¼ in)

19 cm (7½ in)

pebble bag template

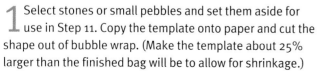

1 Select stones or small pebbles and set them aside for use in Step 11. Copy the template onto paper and cut the shape out of bubble wrap. (Make the template about 25% larger than the finished bag will be to allow for shrinkage.)

2 Place the template in the centre of the reed mat. Starting at the top left corner of the template, lay out a single layer of the dark Shetland wool tops onto the reed mat keeping to the shape of the template, but allowing an extra 2 cm (¾ in) all around. Remove the template from under the fibres and place it on top of the wool layer to check the size.

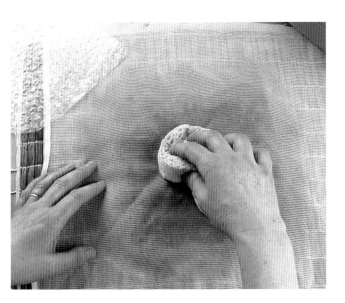

3 Put the template to one side and cover the wool fibres with the net. Using the sponge, damp the fibres gently starting in the centre and working outwards but keeping the edges dry.

4 Remove the net and place the template back onto the wool. Starting at the sides, carefully fold the fibres over so that the edges of the template are covered. Make sure that the wool is pulled tight to this edge so that the sides of the bag will have a clearly defined shape. The top should be folded over last.

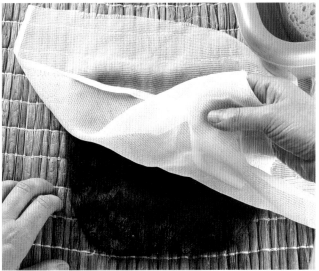

5 Lay a single layer of the dark Shetland wool tops to cover any gap showing, taking care not to go beyond the edges of the bag shape.

6 Cover the wool fibres with the net and gently wet the surface using a sponge. Add a little soap to help settle the fibres. Make sure there are no fibres extending beyond the folded edges.

LAYERING / PEBBLE BAG

7 Repeat the laying out process as before using the light Shetland wool tops, but this time adding two more layers of wool, each at right angles to the previous layer.

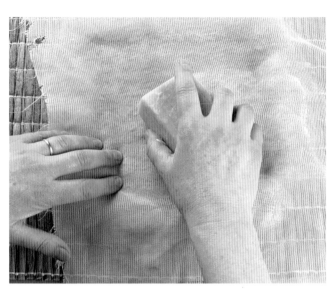

8 Cover the fibres with the net, wet out the fibres, and rub soap over the entire surface. Gently rub the surface until the surface is smooth. Remove the net and carefully turn over the parcel.

9 Pull the fibres over the edges as shown in Step 4 and continue to add fibres as shown in Step 7. Cover with the net, wet out the fibres, and rub soap over the entire surface as shown in Step 8.

10 Remove the net and gently rub the surface until the wool begins to feel firm and holds its shape. You should end up with a neat parcel and there should be no dark wool showing.

11 Place the pebbles onto the bag surface. Position them just below the centre of the bag to allow room for the handles to be cut in Step 19. Leave a small space between each pebble. Cover the pebble area with the silk chiffon square, making sure the pebbles are well within the surface area of the silk.

12 Gently push the wet sponge into the silk with firm dabbing movements to encourage the fabric to become part of the wool base. Make sure there are no puckered areas or folds and that the pebbles are firmly in place. Massage gently around the pebbles to encourage the fibres to travel through the chiffon and hold them in place.

13 Pull tufts from the light Shetland wool tops and lay them over the silk chiffon. It is important to cover the cut edges of the silk completely, but allow the covered pebbles to be seen. (As the wool felts, the silk will become tightly stretched and the pebbles will appear to vanish!)

14 With your fingers, work the wool fibres into the silk chiffon and fold any dry edges over the bag sides and into the wet wool surface. Pay special attention to the area of silk covering the pebbles. Rub the fabric into the wool between the pebbles until it is felted in.

LAYERING / PEBBLE BAG

15 Roll up the bag in the reed mat and roll for two or three minutes. Turn the bag repeatedly during this time so that the final felting is even and the bag maintains its shape. When you can feel the plastic template moving inside the felt parcel, this means the wool is firm and felted and the template can be removed.

16 Make an incision across the top edge with sharp scissors. Take care not to cut too close to each side edge or the opening will become too large.

17 Remove the bubble wrap template. The two contrasting wool shades are now clearly shown. The darker shade acts as a lining to the bag.

18 Continue felting the inside of the bag and pay extra attention to the cut edge of the bag opening, as this will stretch if care is not taken. Add more soap and warm water to speed up the felting process.

19 Once the inside and top edge of the bag is felted, cut slits for the handle. If you want a softer felted edge after cutting the openings, massage the edges gently with soap and water until the cut fibres are matted together.

↓ *Bucket bags can also be made in two contrasting colours, such as the red and black merino fibres used in the example behind the Pebble Bag.*

Layering collection

Be creative with natural objects and special finds by trapping them in layers of fine, coloured silks and felted wools. Experiment with different fabric and wool types, and add embroidery or machine stitching to embellish surfaces further. The layering technique offers a very unusual and painterly approach to felting with fabrics.

⟐··· TIP FOR LAYERING
Take care when using stones or pebbles and avoid those with sharp edges. The fine silk fabric that covers them may tear during the felting process.

Pebble landscape
Above *This sample of felted silk and pebbles makes a lovely decorative textile for a small table or a window sill. It is made using the same technique as the Pebble Bag.*

Green landscape
Right *Glittering pieces of gold-flecked stone are revealed beneath a layer of black silk chiffon. The felted surface is embellished with pockets of machine embroidery.*

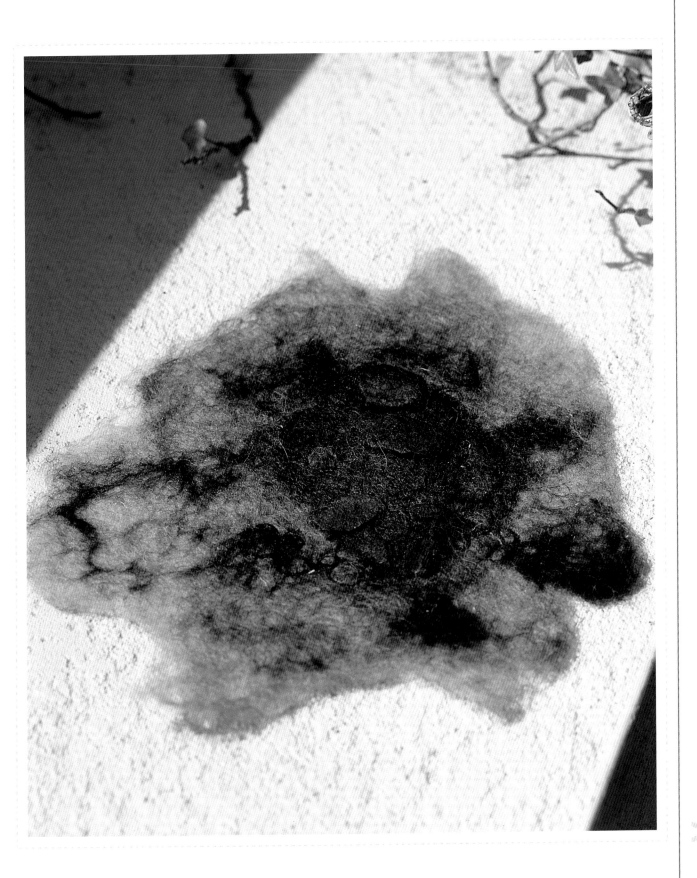

LAYERING / PEBBLE SAMPLES

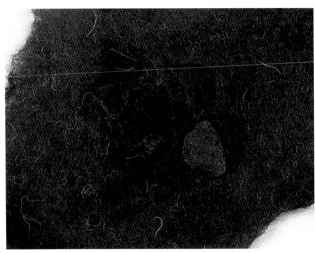

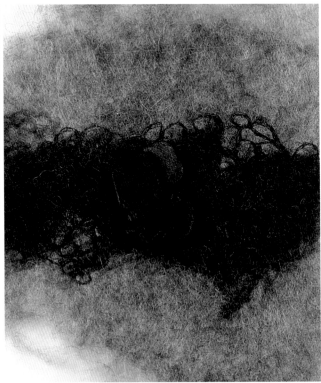

Stone samples

Above, right and below *Subtle contours and shapes are enhanced with machine embroidery over silk in these small landscapes. All the pieces are inspired by nature and feature coloured stones and smooth pebbles collected on my travels.*

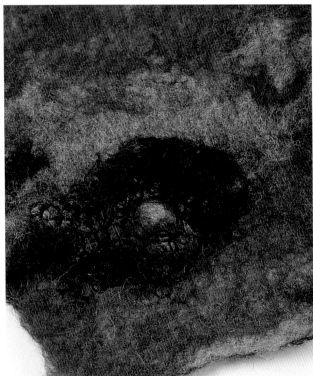

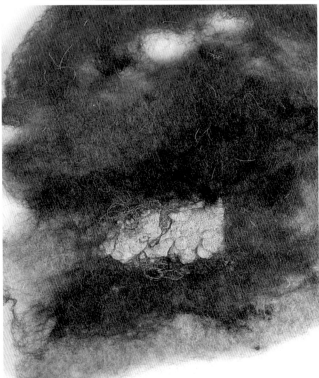

Koi panels

Above *Fine layers of dyed pre-felts, synthetic net and nylon chiffon fabrics were used in this panel to create depth and an underwater feel. The fish were made from separate pre-felts in complementary colours then embedded within the fabric layers to suggest koi in a shadowy setting. Cutting away shaped holes in the fabric can further enhance the shadowy effect of the watery landscape.*

>> LAYERING / MUSLIN SAMPLES

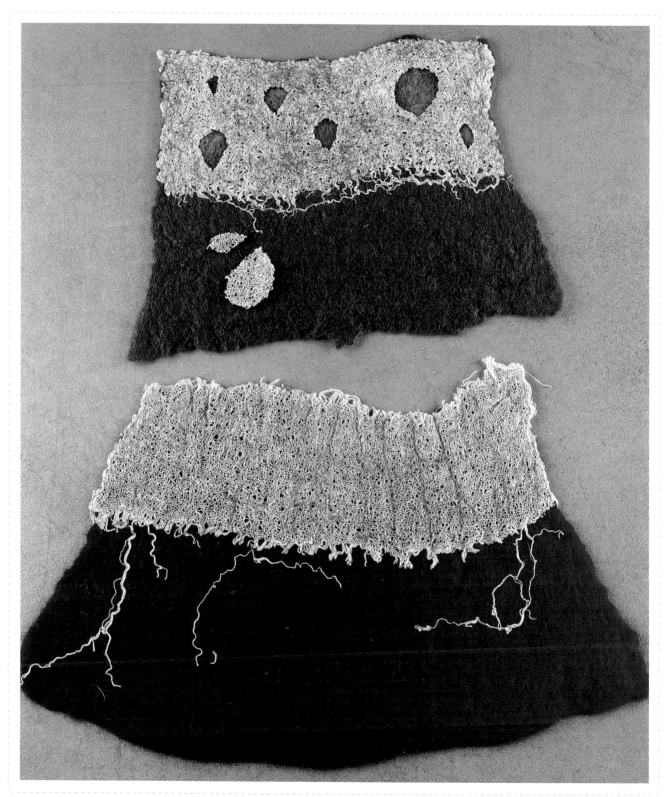

Left *Individual muslin threads and frayed edges can make very attractive decorative effects on plain felted wool surfaces.*

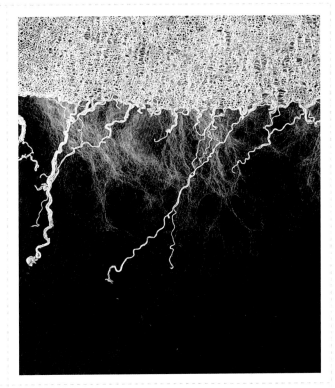

Right *Fine wisps of carded wool fibres and muslin threads contrast with the dark felted background to dramatic effect.*

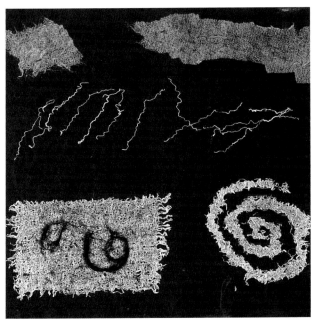

Above *This sampler demonstrates some of the different effects that can be achieved using muslin cloth and threads.*

Above *Subtle pink and cream fibres were combined in this felted muslin cloth.*

>> LAYERING SAMPLES

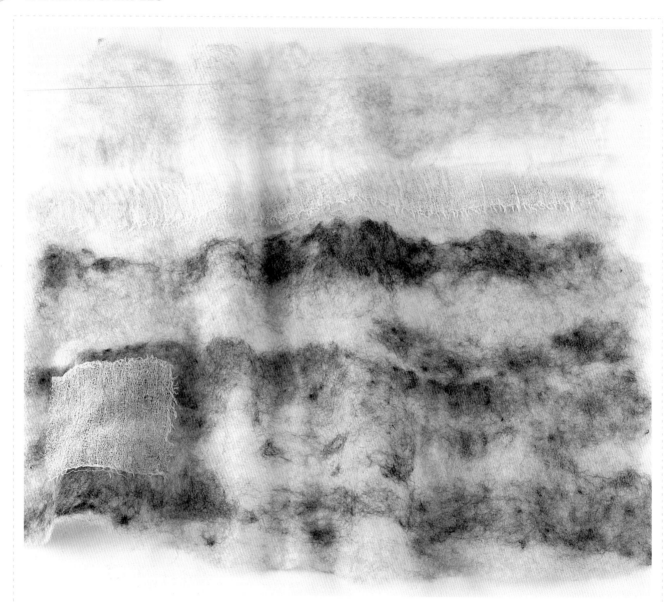

Finn wool landscape

Above *Finn wool has a soft, lustrous quality. It is easy to felt and is particularly good for nuno projects. The Finn sheep is a breed closely related to other Scandinavian sheep. To recreate the landscape, cut strips of muslin in various widths. Hand card the dyed wool fibres into tonal combinations. Place the carded wool fibres alternately with the strips of muslin, making sure there is an overlap of fabric and wool between each layer. Additional muslin shapes may be added to the surface to add interest.*

Bucket bags with layered buttons
Right *Layers of fabric, wool and aluminium foil are tightly felted into a sausage and then sliced to make these fancy buttons. You'll find instructions for making the buttons on page 22, Buttons and Trimmings.*

Bucket bags with button slices
Above *Though not strictly nuno, these fancy swirl buttons have fabric scraps felted into layers of wool to help bind the fibres more tightly and make a firm shape.*

Swirl hat pins and brooch
Above *Use a button slice on a hatpin to decorate hats, scarfs and lapels. A group of slices stitched to a thick felt base can be attached to a brooch pin.*

Nuno 6: Haberdashery

A good selection of haberdashery items will provide endless opportunities to create wonderful lengths of fine and translucent cloth that may be used for elegant evening wraps, window drapes, clothing and much more. A fine and lightweight fabric can be embellished by applying a fine layer of wool tops to either side of the fabric and trapping ribbons, yarns, feathers, leaves, sequins, lace and so on between the fabric and wool layers. Depending on which embellishments you choose, the felting process is usually enough to stabilise the materials without destroying or damaging them. I have found that sequins and glitter work well, but shedding can occur. Leaves and feathers create wonderful effects as light shows through the fabric, but these items are not very robust. Some of the most satisfying materials to use are ribbons, yarns and lace. Natural fibres work well, but synthetic trimmings have the advantage of being abundant and inexpensive. They can be tamed quite readily with a bonding of wool fibre 'glue'.

tools and material

- bubble wrap 2 x 1 metre (6½ x 3½ ft)
- 50 g (1½ oz) white merino wool tops
- length of silk chiffon 180 x 75 cm (5 ft 8 in x 29½ in)
- two types of cream coloured wool yarn: one with slub effect and the other fine ply
- net to cover bubble wrap
- sponge
- olive oil soap
- bowl for water
- scissors
- plastic piping, about 1 metre (3½ ft) long

using natural ingredients

Skeleton leaves and other organic materials can be trapped between layers of fine fabrics and wool, but these are likely to crack and crumble with time, especially in a dry atmosphere. Soaking the felted fabric in a solution of 50:50 water-soluble PVA glue and water will stiffen the cloth and help preserve the leaves. This is particularly helpful for wall hangings and window blinds that are in the sun.

→ *This fine and very beautiful wrap appears translucent in light and drapes well when worn.*

>> **USING THREADS AND YARNS** / SILK YARN WRAP

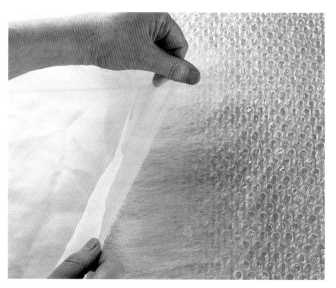

1 Choose your fabrics and yarns. Select wool yarns that have a slight slub effect or crimp. A variety of fine and thick yarns will add interest. Hand-spun yarns can be beautiful and add a special textural quality when used as surface decoration in garments.

2 Place the bubble wrap on your work surface, bubble side up. Lay one fine layer of merino tops to the size of the silk chiffon. Lay the silk chiffon over the fibres.

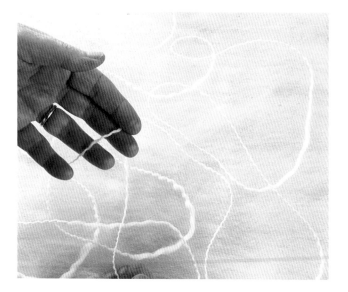

3 Cover the silk chiffon with a fine layer of merino tops. Unwind the wool yarn with the slub effect from the cone and create a random pattern over the surface of the silk and fibres. Cover this with a very fine web of wool pulled from the merino tops. This will help trap and secure the yarns during the felting process.

4 Cover the fibres and yarn with the net and add water and soap using the sponge. Make sure the fibres are thoroughly wetted out.

5 Remove the net and add the second, finer yarn. Cover the yarn with a light, barely visible covering of merino tops. Repeat Step 4: cover with the net and rub soap into the surface with the sponge.

6 Roll up the entire length of fabric around a length of plastic piping, keeping both the net and bubble wrap in place. Roll for several minutes. Unroll and carefully remove the felt and squeeze out excess water. Roll up and repeat without the net.

Rinse the felt carefully in clean water and check the felt. If necessary sponge with warm water, add soap, and continue to roll until the wool and silk chiffon are fully integrated. Leave to dry then press with a warm iron.

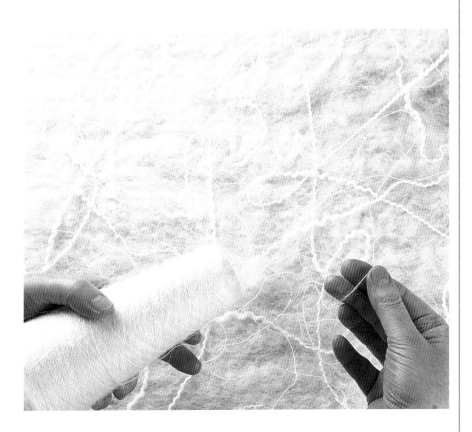

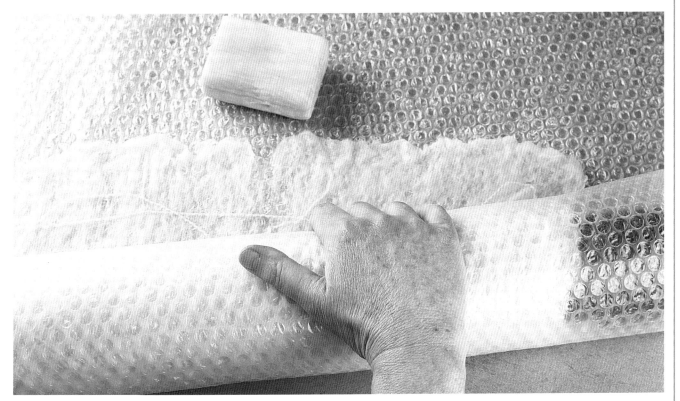

Recycling ideas

Small pieces of trimmings, ribbons and other scraps of materials can be incorporated into unique designs for scarfs and garments. Look out for lace oddments and trimmings at markets, bric-a-brac stalls and charity shops. Discarded scarfs can also be cut up and recycled to form part of gorgeous one-off pieces.

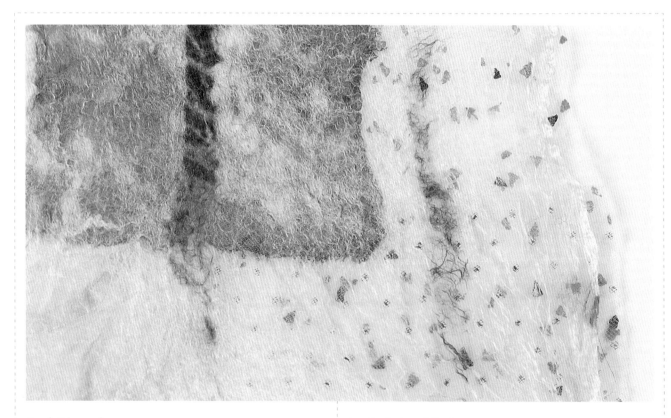

Confetti scarf
Above *Scraps of fabric and ribbon were used to decorate the surface of the pretty Confetti Scarf. A fine web of merino wool placed between the fabric layers created a bond during the felting process.*

Leaf window blind
Right *This transparent and delicate window blind reveals a sprinkling of leaves when the sun shines through. It was made in the same way as the Silk Yarn Wrap on page 112.*

⋯⫶ **TIP FOR HABERDASHERY SAMPLES**
Experiment with wool types: different results can be achieved by changing materials and altering the scale and dimension of a design. Choose Cotswold fleece for a more robust hanging, for example.

≫ HABERDASHERY SAMPLES

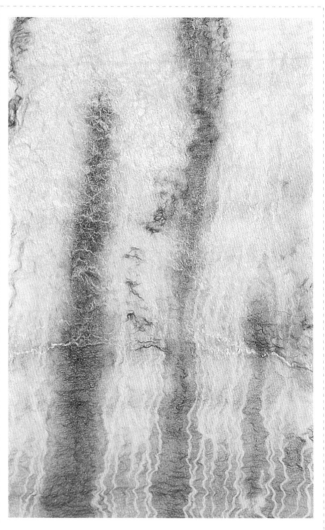

Antique lace scarfs
Above *These sophisticated little scarfs make use of antique lace. The lace is felted into layers of silk chiffon and hand-carded merino and silk fibres. Only one edge of the lace is felted, so a pretty gathered effect is achieved when the wool felts.*

Ribbons
Above *In this fabric sample, the silk chiffon was first dyed with a wrapped resist to give it a ripple effect. The wider areas of dye marks were overlaid with ribbons to create the subtle 'shadows'.*

Shadow play
Right *A jigsaw of fabric layers and ribbon pieces were joined to create this stunning cloth. To make it, overlapping layers of resist dyed fabric pieces were felted together with an almost invisible layer of merino wool used as 'glue'. The same technique can be used to create larger pieces, such as innovative panels or garments.*

Nuno 7: Embellishing

A book such as this one, which discusses methods and techniques of applying fabrics to felted cloth, would not be complete without reference to a new piece of equipment that is now readily available to makers. This fairly recent addition to the domestic craft scene is the embellishing machine or embellisher. An embellishing machine works in exactly the same way as an industrial needlepunch machine, but on a much smaller scale. It resembles a sewing machine that is set up for free embroidery stitch, but without thread. Thanks to its set of five barbed felting needles that punch into the fibres at high speed, fabrics and fibres can be entangled. It is possible to combine loose fibres with felt or other fabric base materials to create instant effects that may also be wet felted, depending on the quality of fabric and finish required. Embellishing is particularly useful for projects requiring detailed and precise decorative effects or to add synthetic materials and fibres that are awkward to felt into wool. Using an embellishing machine to start the bonding process saves time and energy! As a result, innovative designs and mark-making can be achieved very quickly.

As a feltmaker who works entirely with her hands and likes to be in control of the fibres at all stages of the felting process, using a machine has certainly challenged my aesthetics. However, there is much to be recommended with using embellishing machines. As someone who never throws anything away, I have happily created new cloth from scraps of fabrics and wool left over from previous projects. Garments have been re-invented and recycling has never been more rewarding.

→ An old hand-knitted cardigan was transformed by being embellished with merino wool tops in matching colours. The synthetic fancy yarns in the original garment glisten like jewels in the newly embellished mohair surface.

project 1 cushion cover

An excellent way to become acquainted with the embellishing machine is to embed wool fibres into the knitted surface of old woollen garments. It can be very satisfying to watch a new surface emerge; furthermore, the transformation is instant and effortless!

tools and material
- knitted woollen cardigan or sweater
- 50 g (2 oz) coloured merino wool tops that contrast or complement the garment
- embellishing machine
- scissors

>> EMBELLISHING 1 / EMBELLISHED CUSHION COVER

1 Undo the garment seams and cut two 50 x 50 cm (19½ x 19½ in) squares from the knitted fabric. Choose a blend of hand-dyed merino tops to complement the knitted fabric of the garment.

2 Lay a single layer of wool from the merino tops to cover the wrong side of each of the two squares. Using the embellishing machine, punch the wool fibres into each of the knitted surfaces. Add more wool fibres as necessary until the surface is completely covered and a matt surface is achieved.

3 The design or pattern features of the original garment will become entangled with the embellished added fibre. The fabric is now ready to be made into cushions (see Making a Cushion, page 20). Alternatively, wet felting the fabric will give a different feel and look to the fabric. This will also diminish the punctured appearance caused by the needles.

new from old

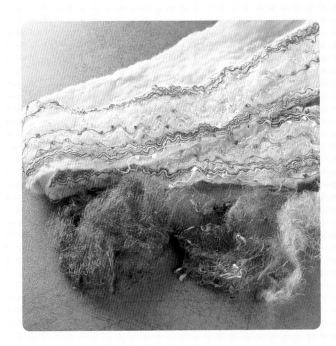

Another good use for the embellishing machine is to create a completely new cloth from waste materials. I often have bags of scrap fabrics and fibres left over from projects. These might include the selvedge cuttings from lengths of fabrics, trimmings, scraps of lace and netting or snipped edges of felt fabric and leftover wool and yarns from dye lots. Pretty much any kind of textile can be used and transformed into magical pieces of new cloth.

← A selection of fibres, yarns and scraps of felt.

project 2 **Gaudi brooches**

By carefully combining scraps you can create a colourful and decorative brooch that has jewel-like qualities. This design was inspired by a visit to the Parc Guell in Barcelona. The wonderful square featuring the artist Gaudi's broken tile designs in the seats and walls gave me ideas for rich jewellery designs and other decorative applications.

tools and material

- leftover coloured merino wool tops that contrast with or complement the fabric scraps
- fabric scraps
- embellishing machine
- scrap of felt to back the brooch
- scissors
- brooch fastening
- needle and thread

EMBELLISHING 2 / EMBELLISHED BROOCHES

1 Finger card the wool fibres and lay these onto larger pieces of felt or pre-felted material. Add fabric scraps. Embellish the surface of these loose fibres to entangle and mesh them together. Keep adding scraps until the cloth becomes firm and stable. This fabric may be wet felted afterwards if desired.

2 Cut a brooch shape from the embellished cloth and place it on a felted base of a contrasting colour. Embellish these two surfaces together so that the recycled materials are completely integrated with the plain felt base.

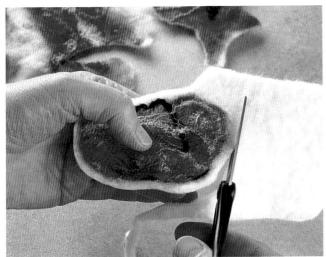

3 Cut around the edge of the brooch shape leaving a small margin of the base felt showing.

4 Finish the piece by hand stitching a brooch fastening to the reverse side.

← Making unique jewellery such as a Gaudi Brooch is a quick and creative way to recycle oddments of felt and scraps of ribbon, lace, silk and yarns.

Using different wools

The embellishing machine offers good opportunities for experimentation with more robust and coarse wool types, such as Herdwick and Swaledale. (See page 15.) It also enables you to use hessian and more closely woven cloths. It is possible to wet felt designs after the materials have been needle punched.

Blue abstract sample
Above *This sample demonstrates the use of cut pre-felt shapes with carded wool embellished onto a woven wool fabric. The cut pieces and wool were placed in random, overlapping layers on the woven surface and embellished with the machine. If small pieces are used in a design, it is a good idea to tack these in place first. The stitches can easily be removed after embellishing the surface.*

Hessian sample

Above top (front) and below (back) *Cut fabrics and hessian were tacked in place before embellishing. Threads from the top fabric layer were punched through the wool and hessian layers. Contrasting colours punctuate the surface to create a distinctive surface. Wet felting can remove some of the regularity of the needle marks as the wool felts into and across the tiny holes made by the needles.*

>>

EMBELLISHED SAMPLES

Flower corsage

Right *The petal shapes of this flower corsage were cut from embellished fabrics created from felt, woven silks and cotton. The slightly frayed edges of the petals help make this an attractive floral decoration that can be pinned onto a lapel, bag or hat. The centre of the corsage is decorated with three small felt balls. The petals and felt balls were hand stitched together and a brooch pin was sewn onto the back.*

> ···⟩ **TIP FOR THE CORSAGE**
>
> To make stamens for the Flower Corsage, roll three or four thin sausage shapes of felt approximately 7 cm (2¾ in) in length. Fold these in half and stitch them into the centre of the flower, open ends upwards. (See page 22 for making felt sausages.)

Embellished sample

Above *These pictures show an embellished sample from the topside (above left) and the underside (above right).*

The underside demonstrates how the coloured threads from the woven silk material have penetrated the layers of wool and fabric to create interesting tonal qualities.

Rose tie

This hand-felted wool tie features a silk flower motif. It was embellished with silk chiffon and selvedge scraps to create texture and a subtle relief surface. The reverse has a flower motif where the embellisher punched fragments of silk into the felt surface. There was no need to line this tie.

Index

Page numbers in italics refer to illustrations. As many materials and techniques are used throughout the book, the page references are intended to direct the reader to substantial entries only.

Acknowledgements

Sincere thanks to the team at Breslich & Foss for their support and encouragement in the production of this book, and particularly Janet Ravenscroft for her initial request to take on the project. Our first meeting was a blind date at Tate Britain on arguably the hottest day during the summer of 2006, with no mobiles to guide us (Janet is a confessed Luddite!) but the response was immediate. How I will miss all those hilarious emails and the wonderful sense of humour during times of self-inflicted anxiety. Also thanks to Shona Wood for her photographic skills and fortitude in coping with sub-zero temperatures in my studio, and to Lisa Tai for her elegant design. To Houdi, Janet's four-legged companion, who danced amongst the wool fibres and provided comic relief. Not forgetting, Ben, my husband, whose computer was never his own and was often seen flinching on hearing me say: 'I'm just going to type a few more words....' Thanks to fellow textile artist Teresa Searle for introducing me to Janet in the first instance! Finally, it's been a privilege to discuss technical issues and concerns with those feltmaking colleagues around the world whose good advice and shared experiences have been invaluable in the writing of this book, which I hope offers a worthy contribution in the development of contemporary feltmaking.

Design by Lisa Tai
Photography Shona Wood
Project management by Janet Ravenscroft
Template by Stephen Dew